10/26/15
$21.95

Retelling
the
Stories
of
Our Lives

Retelling
the
Stories
of
Our Lives

Everyday Narrative Therapy to
Draw Inspiration and
Transform Experience

David Denborough

W. W. Norton & Company
New York • London

Copyright © 2014 by David Denborough

All rights reserved.
Printed in the United States of America
First Edition

For information about permission to reproduce selections from
this book, write to Permissions, W. W. Norton & Company, Inc.
500 Fifth Avenue, New York, NY 10110

For permission about special discounts for bulk purchases, please
contact W. W. Norton Special Sales at specialsales@wwnorton.com
or 800-233-4830

Manufacturing by Quad Graphics Fairfield
Design by MidAtlantic Publishing Services
Production manager: Leeann Graham

Library of Congress Cataloging-in-Publication Data

Denborough, David.
    Retelling the stories of our lives : everyday narrative therapy to
draw inspiration and transform experience / David Denborough.
— First edition.
        pages   cm
    "A Norton Professional Book."
    Includes bibliographical references and index.
    ISBN 978-0-393-70815-8 (pbk.)
1. Narrative therapy. I. Title.
RC489.S74D46 2014
616.89'165—dc23

                            2013031460

ISBN:978-0-393-70815-8 (pbk.)

W. W. Norton & Company, Inc., 500 Fifth Avenue, New York, N.Y.
10110
                    www.wwnorton.com
W. W. Norton & Company Ltd., Castle House, 75/76 Wells Street,
London W1T 3QT

1 2 3 4 5 6 7 8 9 0

Contents

    Picture?   271

    Epilogue   Looking Back, Looking Forward   289

    References   293

    Index   299

Preface

Dear Reader,

Our lives and their pathways are not fixed in stone; instead they are shaped by story. The ways in which we understand and share the stories of our lives therefore make all the difference. If we tell stories that emphasize only desolation, then we become weaker. Alternatively, we can tell our stories in ways that make us stronger, in ways that soothe the losses, in ways that ease sorrow.

In the pages that follow, I will share stories with you from different parts of the world—from individuals, groups, and communities who are rewriting the stories of their lives. And I will ask you questions about the stories of your life—about the central characters, the plots, the key scenes, even the soundtrack.

I am interested in why you have picked up this book. Perhaps you are going through hard times or long for something to be different in life, or perhaps you have a friend or family member whom you dearly want to help. I don't know the stories of your life. I do know, however, that with the right questions and the right audience, the stories of our lives can be transformed.

When our lives have been more tragedy than triumph, too often this is because other people have written the stories that influence our lives, or because broader powers such as sexism, violence, racism, or poverty have become the authors of the storylines of our identity. This is a book about revising these life stories and writing our own.

I spend many of my days meeting with people in situations of great hardship. I often say that I get to see the best and the worst of the world. I witness the profound harm and injustice that people do to people. And I get to meet children, young people, and adults who are reclaiming their lives and protecting what is important to them. There is nothing more significant to me than this reclamation. Sometimes it takes generations to change storylines; in other situations it can take a single conversation.

The book you are holding in your hands has been written to assist individuals, friends, families, and communities in rewriting and retelling the stories of their lives. There are two different ways to use it.

Perhaps you will read it privately. Just you, these pages, and a pen, so that you can respond to the questions and exercises that are included throughout. One of the beauties of a book is the exquisite privacy and intimacy between the reader and the text. You may wish to share with these pages stories that you have never told others. If so—well, that's one of the reasons this book was written.

Alternatively, you may wish to share this book with a friend, complete the exercises together, and ask each other the questions that are posed throughout. You could do this via letter, online, via Skype, via email, via Facebook, or over a meal.

Whichever way you choose, I hope this book provides new options for ways of talking about your life and the lives of your friends and family members.

The History of This Book

The idea for this book emerged some years ago in conversations and collaborations with Michael White, who, alongside his intellectual "brother" David Epston, created the field of narrative therapy.[1] Michael was an enchanting therapist, writer, and teacher. His ideas changed the direction of my life and the lives of many others. I worked alongside Michael for close to fifteen years, in writing projects and community assignments.[2] While he was finishing his book *Maps of Narrative Practice*, we planned to coauthor a book to introduce narrative ideas to a general audience. While we hadn't planned its contents, we knew what we hoped it would achieve.

For a number of reasons, our collaboration on this book never had a chance. Michael White died in 2008, and we had not worked closely together in the year before his passing. After his death, one of the most pressing concerns was to make available a collection of Michael's previously unpublished papers. In 2011, in collaboration with Cheryl White, David Epston, Jill Freedman, and the Michael White Archive at Dulwich Centre (www.dulwichcentre.com.au/michael-white-archive.html), we put together an edited collection titled *Narrative Practice: Continuing the Conversations* (W. W. Norton).

Only now has it been possible to return to the earlier hope of a book introducing narrative ideas to a general audience. While sadly not coauthored with Michael as planned, this book has involved collaboration with the Michael White Archive at Dulwich Centre. Within these pages you will find many sparkling stories of Michael's therapeutic conversations. Also included here are extracts of writings that Dulwich Centre has published over the last thirty years.[3] It has been a joy to be immersed in these writings again and to imagine people reading them for the first time. The ideas and stories within this book have been like friends to me over the last two decades, and I hope they are good company for you also.

Before Michael died, the only writing that had been done in relation to this book was a draft preface. Within it, Michael described his hopes for this book:

> This book is not about imposing new stories on people's lives or giving advice. Instead, this book invites readers to take a new look at their own lives and to find a new significance in events often neglected, to find sparkling actions that are often discounted, to find fascination in experiences previously overlooked, and to find solutions to problems and predicaments in landscapes often previously considered bereft. . . . This will provide the reader with options in knowing how to go forward.

I hope this remains true.

Notes

1. It was David Epston and Cheryl White who first encouraged Michael White to explore the "story" or "narrative" metaphor in therapy. For more about this history, see Denborough, 2009. For more information about narrative therapy, see www.dulwich centre.com.au/common-questions-narrative-therapy.html
2. I have worked for the last twenty years within the field of narrative therapy and community work. Many of my recent projects with Dulwich Centre Foundation have been with groups and

communities in different parts of the world who have experienced profound hardship. Throughout these projects, we have needed to adapt narrative therapy ideas in order to make them widely accessible. This book draws upon these experiences.

3. The writings published by Dulwich Centre have been adapted with permission for use in this book.

Acknowledgments

MANY PEOPLE HAVE made this book possible. I would particularly like to acknowledge Deborah Malmud at W. W. Norton, who never gave up on the idea of this book and offered significant editorial guidance. Sophie Hagen and Rachel Keith also made meaningful contributions to the publishing process. Leigh Corrigan and Kate le Dan provided artwork. Mike Bowers took the photograph included on page 166.

In addition, the following people offered invaluable feed-back on earlier drafts: Cheryl White, Jill Freedman, Mary Heath, David Epston, Daria Kutuzova, David Newman, Ruth Pluznick, Amy Druker, Loree Stout, Dale Andersen-Giberson, Susanna Chamberlain, Kaylene Graham, Meredith Oliver, and Erica Denborough.

I would like to make a special acknowledgment to Kaethe Weingarten who provided detailed feedback on this manuscript. Not only is Kaethe a significant figure in the family therapy field with her work in three realms—illness narratives, trauma, and witnessing—she is also a highly skilled editor.

Within these pages you will read stories of work from Jussey Verco, Silent Too Long, Kate, Ncazelo Ncube, the counselors of Ibuka, Sue Mann, Carolyn Markey, Chris Dotman, Margaret Hayward, Eileen Hurley, Angel Yuen, the Alzheimer's Australia Vic Community Advisory Group, Nihaya Abu-Rayyan, Power to Our Journeys, Chris McLean, Sue Mitchell, the ACT Mental Health Consumers Network, Carolynanha Johnson, Julie Moss, and Lisa Berndt. Without their contributions, this book would not exist.

Through a collective effort, I hope we have managed to achieve what Michael and I set out to do some years ago.

Retelling
the
Stories
of
Our Lives

Part One

CHAPTER 1

A Life of Stories

WHO WE ARE and what we do are influenced by the stories that we tell about ourselves. While we can't always change the stories that others have about us, we can influence the stories we tell about ourselves and those we care about. And we can, with care, rework or rewrite storylines of identity. Let me explain with a story.

Picture a thirteen-year-old boy sitting on the top of a mountain ridge. He's at a school camp, but he's on his own. All the other boys are off on a hike that's supposed to take them a couple of nights. This boy couldn't join them because he'd grown up with serious asthma. As an even smaller child, during the first four years of his life, he didn't speak like "normal" kids. It wasn't until he was about four and a half that people could understand all his words.

At this point in the story, you are probably painting a particular picture of this young thirteen-year-old sitting on the top of a mountain ridge by himself. You are probably linking a couple of events in his life into a storyline (see Figure 1.1).

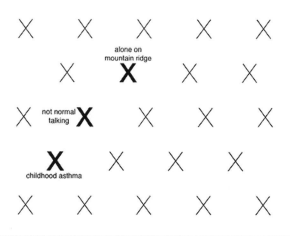

Figure 1.1. Life events.

This is what we do in life. We take certain events and then link them together into a plot or theme. And this plot or theme about our lives then shapes our identities—who we are. In thinking about the three events that I have told you about this boy, what theme have you identified? My guess is it might be something like "lonely boy" or "a different sort of child" (see Figure 1.2).

But that's because I have selected certain events to tell you first. What if I added three more events:

1. That day on the ridge, the thirteen-year-old boy wrote his first song. He played air guitar and sang it to the mountains and to his friends (members of his rugby team) when they returned from their hike.

2. As a small child, this boy had often gone on walks with his dad, and whenever they got to the top of a hill his father would sing, "I'm on top of the world, looking down on cre-

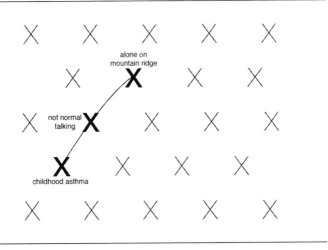

Figure 1.2. Linking events into a good storyline: "Lonely boy."

ation, and the only explanation I can find is the love I have found ever since you've been around, that has put me right on top of the world!"

3. As a small child, the boy's mother had always found a way to decipher his "unique language" and understand him. The boy has no memory of feeling misunderstood.

With these three new events added, suddenly the storyline or plot of this boy's life changes too. The first events I told you about are still true, but with these other events surrounding them, their meanings have changed).

What theme or storyline would you give to this boy's life now? Well, actually, what matters most is the storyline he gives to these events and the storyline that is supported and reflected by those he knows and whose opinions he values. As you may have guessed, these are events from my life.

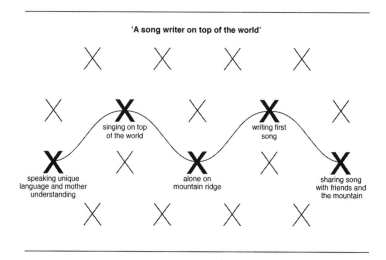

Figure 1.3. Linking alternative events into a second storyline: "A songwriter on top of the world."

If I were to name this second storyline, a storyline I much prefer, I think I'd give it the name "A songwriter on top of the world." (See Figure 1.3.)

I have shared these stories to demonstrate how our lives are shaped by story. There are many different events in our lives, but only some of them get formed into the storylines of our identities. Whatever storyline we have about our lives makes a difference in who we are and how we act. If I believed I was "lonely boy," and if other people related to me as if I was "lonely boy," my life would be very different than it would be if I saw myself—and others saw me—as "a songwriter on top of the world." "Lonely boy" can be seen as a "problem story," whereas "a songwriter on top of the world" can be seen as a "preferred story."

The aim of this book is to share with you questions, tools, and ideas to generate preferred stories of your life and to create preferred stories of the lives of those you care about. In all of our lives, there will be events that make us cringe, those that bring heartache, those that bring sorrow, those that bring shame. If those moments are all linked together into a story-line, we can feel truly hopeless about life. But in all of our lives, there will also be events or small moments of beauty, or kindness, or respite, or escape, or defiance. When these events are linked together to tell a story about us, then life becomes easier to live. This book is about creating storylines of our lives that we can respect and that we can live with.

Let me show you how this relates to Vanessa's life.[1]

Changing the Headline

Things have been difficult in Vanessa's life recently, especially since she lost her apartment in the housing crisis two years ago. Sometimes, these days, especially when she's finding it difficult to pay the rent for her current accommodations, the words of her ex-husband ring in her ears: "You're good for nothing!" Whenever this phrase visits Vanessa, she instantly thinks of all the things she has done badly in her life and all the people she has disappointed. As her ex-husband's words echo in her mind, she feels as if she's shriveling inside.

In those moments, it's as if the phrase "You're Good for Nothing" becomes the headline of the story of Vanessa's life. She sees those words as if they are written in big, bold lettering, visible to everyone, and she feels that once people have read that headline, it will shape everything they think about her.

But this is not "the truth" of Vanessa's life; it's one story. It's one story told by an abusive ex-husband and supported by current economic hard times. There are many other storylines of Vanessa's life, and her sister, Salome, knows this all too well.

Salome often calls Vanessa "the kindest person I know." The reason for this goes back to when they were in high school together. Vanessa, though two years older, was always there for Salome—checking in every lunch hour, raising her spirits, introducing her to others, and telling off those who would give Salome a hard time because she walked and sounded different from everyone else.

Recently, whenever Vanessa has begun to feel dominated by the "good for nothing" story, she has phoned her sister. In their laughter together, they have been writing a different headline.

Storytelling Rights

The stories we tell about ourselves are not created in a vacuum. All too often, the stories we believe about ourselves have been written by others. For instance, for those who experienced abuse as children, the perspective of the abuser often remains present in the critical thoughts they continue to have about themselves. Similarly, sexism and racism contribute to negative storylines about women and people of color. Too often, the stories of people's lives are told through abusive, racist, sexist, or homophobic lenses.

In all of these situations, it can be significant to consider your storytelling rights.[2] Storytelling rights are not as well-known as other forms of rights, but they are important. One of the first steps in rewriting the stories of your identity may require you to reclaim the storytelling rights over your own life.

Some time ago, when collaborating with human rights organizations, I created what I call the "Charter of Storytelling Rights," which consists of seven key articles (I use the term *article* because that's what is used in the Universal Declaration of Human Rights):

- **Article 1.** Everyone has the right to define their experiences and problems in their own words and terms.

- **Article 2.** Everyone has the right to have their life understood in the context of what they have been through and in the context of their relationships with others.

- **Article 3.** Everyone has the right to invite others who are important to them to be involved in the process of reclaiming their life from the effects of hardship.

- **Article 4.** Everyone has the right not to have problems caused by trauma and injustice located inside them, internally, as if there were some deficit in them. The person is not the problem; the problem is the problem. (See Chapter Two).

- **Article 5.** Everyone has the right to have their responses to hard times acknowledged. No one is a passive recipient of hardship. People always respond. People always protest injustice.

- **Article 6.** Everyone has the right to have their skills and knowledge of survival respected, honored, and acknowledged.

- **Article 7.** Everyone has the right to know and experience that what they have learned through hard times can make a contribution to the lives of others in similar situations.

Like any form of rights, storytelling rights need defending and sometimes reclaiming. If we are going to revise the storylines of our lives, there will be times when it is necessary to reclaim and defend storytelling rights when they have been violated. For instance, for Vanessa to move the headline for her life from "Good for Nothing" to "The Kindest Person I Know," she will need to reclaim her right to define her experiences and problems in her own words and terms (Article 1). She will also need to reclaim her right to have her life understood in the context of what she has been through (Article 2), including escaping from an abusive marriage and dealing with the current economic downturn.

Consider for a moment whether there have been times when you stood up for the storytelling rights of others. Have there been times when someone has been speaking about another person, or a group of other people, and you have thought, "It's not right that you are speaking for or about that person. That person should be able to speak for him- or herself"? Have there been times when you have said something or done something that has made it possible for someone to speak for him- or herself rather than be spoken for?

And have there been times when you have tried to claim your own storytelling rights in relation to your life? Have others tried to define what is wrong about your life, or tried to offer solutions that might work for their life but would not work for yours? And have you protested this in some way, even if it was a silent protest?

A Safe Place From Which to Speak Our Stories

Alongside considering, defending, and reclaiming storytelling rights for ourselves and others, it's also important to consider when we tell certain stories of our lives and to whom.

The next chapter focuses on ways of speaking about the problems, difficulties, or hardships of our lives. Before we speak about such hardships, however, it can be significant to develop what is called a "riverbank" position in relation to our own lives.[3] If our life is in turmoil, it's like a river, fast flowing and full of hazards and dangers. If we're in the middle of a fast-flowing river, it may not be the time to talk about those hazards or dangers. Instead, all our efforts may need to go into immediate survival. We need to find a way to step out of the turmoil and the fast-flowing water and up onto the riverbank, where we can then look down upon our own life.

One means of creating such a riverbank position is called the "Tree of Life." This way of looking at our lives originated in Zimbabwe. Ncazelo Ncube, a Zimbabwean/South African psychologist, and I worked together to develop a way to assist people struggling with many losses associated with HIV/ AIDS.[4] The Tree of Life is now being used in many contexts throughout the world. Before we move on to the next chapter, I'd like to invite you to create your own Tree of Life. This is a process you can do by yourself or with others. If there is someone else you know who is also interested in retelling and rewriting the stories of their life, perhaps you could do this process together.

The first step involves drawing a tree. It can be any sort of tree, preferably one that brings with it some sort of positive association. Think for a moment of any trees that are linked to good memories in your own life, and then draw such a tree. If you really struggle with drawing (as I do!), you can use the template in Figure 1.4. If you choose to use the template, do something to make it your own, perhaps by coloring it in

Figure 1.4. Tree of Life template.

ways that will link it to a particular tree from your memory. It's important that the drawing include roots, ground, trunk, branches, leaves, fruits, and seeds. You can add extras, but you'll need each of the components mentioned, because they will represent certain aspects of your life.

The Roots: Where We Come From

The roots of the tree are your prompt to write down where you come from (i.e., village, town, country); your language; your culture; those who have taught you the most in life; your favorite place; your favorite song or dance. You may also include any club or association you belong to or any sporting team you support. Write these on the roots of your tree. You can also include photographs or images. Don't spend too long on the roots to start with (five to seven minutes). You can return to the roots later if need be.

The Ground: What We Choose to Do

The ground represents some of the activities that you choose to do in the course of a week—just regular things, but things that you choose to do (rather than things you are forced to do).

The Trunk: What We Care About and Our Skills

The trunk represents what you value. Have a look back at the ground—what you choose to do during the week. Why do you choose to do these things? What is it that you care about?

You may also place on the trunk the skills and abilities you have demonstrated in your life. These may involve physical accomplishments, areas of practical experience (like cleaning), or skills of caring, kindness, honesty, and so forth. They don't have to be in any way grand. In fact, it's better if they're not.

Sometimes it's hard to think about what to include on your trunk. It can be easier if we ask ourselves, what would a particular friend (or someone who cares about me) say about me? Or we can consider whether we have any ability or know-how that flows from our roots or ground. But we don't have to include only our own individual values, skills, and abilities. We might include something that our community or a group we belong to cares about, or something that our group of friends is good at.

Try to include a diversity of things on your trunk. Then, looking down at your trunk, try to trace the history of each of the things you care about, the things you give value to, your skills and abilities. Whom did you learn this value or skill from? How long has it been important to you? Where did it come from? In responding to these questions, you may think of something or someone to add to your roots. In this way, you start to build connections between different parts of your Tree of Life.

The Branches: Our Horizons

The branches of the tree represent shared hopes, dreams, and wishes. These are not necessarily hopes that you have for your own life. They may be hopes you have for others or for your community. If you can, however, include a hope or wish that you have in relation to your own life. This may be something you are hoping for in relation to the coming week-end, or a dream about the distant future. If possible, include on different branches some longer- and some shorter-term wishes for your life and the lives of others. It's then possible to trace the history of these hopes and desires. How long have you had these hopes? Where did they come from? How have you held on to them? Did anyone introduce you to these hopes or help you to hold on to them? As you consider these questions, you may be inspired to make additions to your trunk or roots.

Leaves of the Tree: Those Who Are Significant to Us

The leaves of the Tree of Life represent those who are significant to you (in a good way). These may be people who are close to you or who have influenced you directly. You may also include heroes on the leaves of your tree, or acknowledge pets and invisible friends.

It's particularly important that those who are no longer alive are still included on our Tree of Life. If someone has been good to us, their legacy remains in our lives (see Chapter 8).

If you wish to include on your leaves people who have passed away, these extra questions may be helpful:

- Did you have good times with this person? If so, write about one of these times next to their leaf.

- What was significant to you about this person? Write this next to their leaf.

- Would this person appreciate that you remember them? And that you put them on your tree?

Fruits: Legacies Bequeathed to Us

The fruits represent gifts that have been passed on to you, or contributions others have made to your life. Look back over the people and other figures you named on the leaves of your tree. Consider what legacies they have passed on to you. These may include gifts like patience or courage. Or they may be material gifts that have been significant to you.

Flowers and Seeds: Legacies We Wish to Leave

The flowers and seeds of the tree represent gifts or legacies that you wish to pass on to others. These may be similar to the gifts you have been offered yourself. Alternatively, they may be things you were never offered in your lifetime and that you wish to offer somebody else. You may have learned the value of certain gifts precisely because you did not have access to them. Consider the legacies you wish to leave and write them next to the flowers and seeds of the tree.

An Optional Theme

There is one optional addition to the Tree of Life that I wish to mention here. It was created by Margaret Hayward, who was participating in a Tree of Life workshop for women who had experienced domestic violence.[5] As she created her tree, Margaret invented something significant, which she describes here (see Figure 1.5):

> When I did my Tree of Life painting, I could not think of a place to put my mother or husband in my Tree of Life, as they were the ones in my life that mentally abused me. Usually on our trees we put the supportive people, pets, and idols that have been important in our lives. This left me no place to put my mom and husband. So I invented a place and called it the "compost heap" as a way to include them in my life, but on my terms. The compost heap is a place where they can no longer abuse me. When they passed, I had nowhere to put them. They didn't fit into the heart of my tree. Looking at my picture, there was something missing. Everybody else that I loved was in full view on the tree. So I invented the compost heap and placed my mother and husband there. By doing so I lifted the hurt from my heart, and I was able to move on. Compost heaps transform rotten stuff into rich and nourishing fertilizer for our lives.

Making Connections

After you have created your Tree of Life, take another look and see if you can make any connections between different

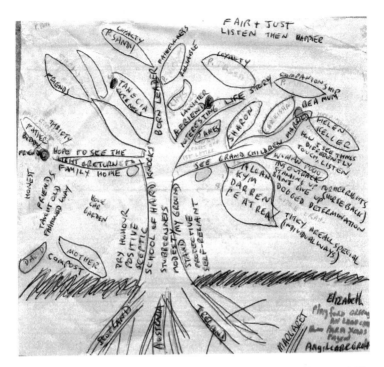

Figure 1.5. Margaret's Tree of Life (see compost heap on bottom left).

parts of the tree. Are the roots, trunk, and branches linked in any way?

If you are doing this exercise with somebody else, have a good look at what they placed on their trunk. First, choose one or two of these themes and ask them to tell you a story about them. You might say, for instance, "Can you tell me about how you value 'honesty' or 'friendship' or how you try to be 'sincere' or 'caring'? Can you tell me about a time when this was significant to you?" Second, ask your friend the same kinds of questions you asked yourself when you filled in your own tree trunk: "Please tell me about the history of this value or skill in your life. Whom did you learn it from? Whom did you learn it with? What is the foundation or the roots of this value or skill in your life?"

As both of you consider these questions, perhaps your friend will mention something that is already listed in the roots of their tree. If not, perhaps it would be good to add it to their roots. It may also link with people who are mentioned on the leaves of their tree.

Making links between what you care about in life, your skills, your hopes and dreams, who is significant to you, and the gifts you have received and wish to pass on is a process of creating a particular "storyline" of your life. This is not a storyline about problems. This storyline—this Tree of Life—is about what you give value to, what you stand for in life. This is a preferred storyline.

Vanessa's Tree of Life

When Vanessa created her Tree of Life, she did so in the company of her sister, Salome. She started with the leaves, and there she included Salome; her niece, Rebecca; her grandparents (who were no longer alive); her mother; a number of friends; and a beloved dog. Not surprisingly, she then placed her ex-husband in a carefully constructed compost heap. Along the ground, Vanessa described some of her weekly activities, including calling Salome, working as a receptionist, caring for her niece, and volunteering at the neighborhood care center for the elderly, where she sometimes draws sketches of the residents to give to their families.

At first, Vanessa found it difficult to think about what to put on the trunk of her tree. What was it that she cared about in life? What were her skills and abilities? But after Vanessa and Salome looked together at who was on the leaves of her tree and what she chose to do each week, she filled her trunk with:

"Drawing"
"Laughing and making people laugh"
"Kindness for family"

Salome suggested that Vanessa include "stubborn strength." After they shared a laugh, Vanessa wrote this down as well.

This was when the process started to get more interesting for both Vanessa and Salome. Where did these skills and values come from? Who had introduced them to Vanessa? What was their history? Vanessa had never thought about this before, but it wasn't long before she and Salome were talking about their grandmother, Nonna. Salome and Vanessa's father had died when they were both very young, which meant that their mother had to work to support the family. It was Nonna who had raised them, and when Salome asked Vanessa where her stubborn strength and kindness had come from, they both immediately realized that these were their grandmother's legacy. They wrote Nonna's name in the roots of Vanessa's tree. Vanessa also wrote in her roots the name of the neighborhood where they had grown up and the playground where Nonna had taken the two of them every day when she needed to get out of the apartment. Salome and Vanessa had not talked about that playground or their times with Nonna for some time.

"Drawing" had a different history, one Salome had never known. Vanessa had gotten through her own hard times at school by drawing people's faces, and she had been encouraged in this endeavor by one of her teachers. In recalling those times, Vanessa placed the teacher's name on an additional leaf.

The history of laughter and making people laugh? Well, Vanessa said, that came from her relationship with Salome. And so, when she turned to the fruits of her tree, Vanessa thought instantly of Salome and wrote down "the gift of laughter" and "the gift of Salome saying, 'You are kindest person I know.'" In fact, Vanessa decided to name her tree "The Kindest Tree Salome Knows."

Finally, they turned to the seeds, the gifts that Vanessa now wished to pass on to others. These, she said, included "acceptance" and "my time." Through making her Tree of Life, Vanessa had come to recognize that these were gifts that Nonna had shared with her, and now she wanted to continue this legacy.

Let's now consider how Vanessa's Tree of Life represents a preferred storyline of her identity.

Rewriting Storylines of Identity

As we saw above, Vanessa's life is sometimes influenced by a problematic storyline, or headline "Good for Nothing" (see Figure 1.6).

This negative headline has real effects on Vanessa's life. When problem storylines take over, it's as if our life—our identity—has become a problem. This is made worse if other people in our lives keep reinforcing the negative storyline, or if sexism, racism, or the "voice of abuse" gives further strength to the problem story.

Through creating a Tree of Life, Vanessa started to tell an alternate storyline of her identity. Just as "a songwriter on top of the world" represented a preferred storyline in my life at

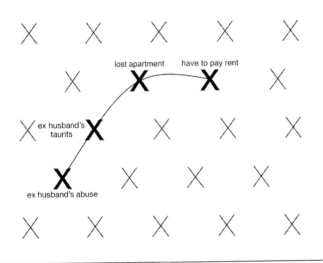

Figure 1.6. *The "good for nothing" storyline of Vanessa's life.*

thirteen, "the kindest person I know" represents a preferred storyline for Vanessa (see Figure 1.7).

As you create your own Tree of Life, and as you work your way through the chapters of the book, I hope you will generate new "headlines" for your life, new storylines for your identity. As we retell and rewrite the stories of life, the facts of our lives won't change, but their meanings can change. Which events are emphasized can change. And if the story we tell about ourselves changes, it will influence what becomes possible for us in the future.

Looking Back, Looking Forward

In this chapter, we've considered how our lives are influenced by the stories we tell about ourselves. We've acknowledged our

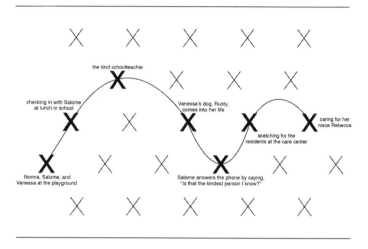

Figure 1.7. *The "kindest person I know" storyline of Vanessa's life.*

storytelling rights and examined whether some of these need to be reclaimed. And we've created a safe place from which to speak our stories through the metaphor of the Tree of Life.

Next, let's consider ways of understanding and talking about the problems we may be up against. As we do so, it's vital that we recognize that we are not our problems. The person is not the problem; the problem is the problem.

Notes

1. Vanessa is a composite character.
2. David Epston and Stephen Madigan introduced the concept of storytelling rights, which I then developed into the charter described in this chapter.
3. Caleb Wakhungu from the Mt. Elgon Self-Help Community Project (www.mt-elgonproject.org) introduced the metaphor of "the riverbank position" during a workshop by Michael White.

4. The Tree of Life narrative approach was developed by Ncazelo Ncube and David Denborough through a collaboration between the Regional Psychosocial Support Initiative (REPSSI) and the Dulwich Centre Foundation. The team that traveled to Zimbabwe, where the Tree of Life approach was developed, consisted of Michael White, Cheryl White, Shona Russell, and David Denborough. For more information about the Tree of Life, see www.dulwichcentre.com.au/tree-of-life.html

5. Margaret Hayward's invention of the compost heap took place during a Tree of Life group facilitated by Jennifer Swan at Anglicare in Adelaide, South Australia. To read more about this group, see www.dulwichcentre.com.au/tree-of-life-womens-group.pdf

CHAPTER 2

We Are Not Our Problems

WHEN IT COMES to retelling and rewriting the stories of our lives, it makes a real difference how we talk about the problems in our lives. If we come to believe that we *are* the problem and that there is something wrong with us, then it becomes very difficult to take action. All we can do is take action against ourselves.

Unfortunately, it's very common to hear ways of speaking that make it sound as if the person is the problem, such as, "He's a bad kid," "Lucy's depressed," "Bill's schizophrenic." And all too often we think about ourselves in these ways too, for example:

- I'm a bad mom.
- I'm useless.
- I'm not smart enough; I'll never finish school.
- I have an addictive personality.
- I have all this anger in me because of what happened to me as a kid.

In each of these descriptions, the person is the problem, and if we think of ourselves as the problem, it can be really difficult to know what to do. It can also be demoralizing. It's particularly easy to come to believe that we are a problem if the influence of sexism, racism, or abuse is around.

This common way of understanding problems as located *inside* people is called "internalizing problems."

Sometimes problems are also internalized in couples or groups of people:

- We've always been bad communicators.
- Our community is hopeless.

There is, however, a different way of understanding life and problems. This alternative way is called "externalizing problems" and is summed up in the phrase "The person is not the problem; the problem is the problem" (White, 1984, 2007).[1] In this way of thinking, the person and the problem are not the same thing (see Figure 2.1).[2] For example, in the following table, contrast the internalized descriptions on the left with the externalized descriptions on the right.[3]

On the right-hand side are externalized descriptions of the problem. Through them, some space is created between the

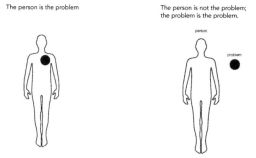

Figure 2.1. Externalizing problems.

The person is the problem.	The person is not the problem; the problem is the problem.
He's a bad kid.	*Trouble* is really following that kid around.
Lucy's a depressed person.	Lucy says she's been in a *fog of depression* since her mother died.
I'm useless.	The *feeling of uselessness* is strongest when I'm in the classroom.
Bill's schizophrenic.	Bill says the *hostile voices* (of schizophrenia) try to convince him that he is worthless.
Our community is hopeless.	*Hope* can be hard to find around here, particularly when there have been so many losses in the community.

person and the problem. This process of separating ourselves from problems makes it possible for us to begin to revise our relationship with the problems.

Sometimes people think that saying, "The child is not the problem; it's his mother that's the problem" is externalizing. It's not! That's just blaming someone else—moving the location of the problem from within one person to within another (see Figure 2.2). It also sounds a lot like mother-blame, which is all too common.

Instead, externalizing is a principle or a philosophy that refuses to locate problems inside people (see Figure 2.3). This way of thinking refuses to pathologize people. Instead, we can

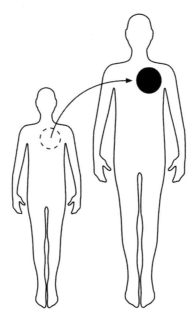

Figure 2.2. This is not externalizing.

acknowledge that problems have histories. They are created over time. And often problems are affected by broader factors, like poverty, racism, and sexism.

This is not to diminish the seriousness of the problem or its effects. Many people struggle with the effects of overwhelming hardship. This makes it all the more important that we speak about these problems and understand them in ways that are separate from the person. The person is not the problem; the problem is the problem.

Externalizing the Problem

It can be difficult at first to externalize the problem and achieve some sense of distance from it. This is particularly true when we have become convinced that we are the problem.

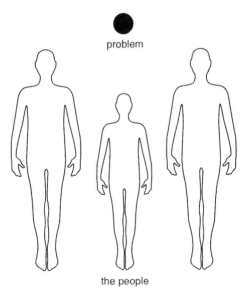

problem

the people

Figure 2.3. The person is not the problem; the problem is the problem.

Take Daniel's situation, for example. The following story, as told by Michael White (2004a), conveys the experience of Daniel and his parents.

Daniel, a sad-looking boy of eleven years of age, was brought to see me by his parents, Tom and Lucy, who were at their wits' end. According to them, Daniel was "bringing trouble down" on their lives in every way imaginable. He had been expelled from two schools and was now suspended from a third. He was in trouble with the police, with neighbors, with the parents of his peers, and he was creating havoc at home as well. As I listened to these details, it was clear to me that Lucy and Tom were attributing very sinister motives to Daniel's actions. In fact, their account of these events was laced with a range of highly negative conclusions about Daniel, and these were painful for me to hear. Among other things, they had concluded that he was "out to destroy the family," that he was a "worthless good-for-nothing," "useless to himself and everyone else," and a "dead loss when it came to efforts to do anything for him." Daniel's response to all of this seemed one of studied indifference. He just sat there, neither confirming nor protesting this account of his life and identity. But I had the sense that he agreed with these very negative conclusions.

I said that on hearing these details I was developing some appreciation of just how frustrating the situation must be. Tom responded to this by exclaiming, "And you don't even know the half of it yet!" My response: "Would it be okay, then, if I asked some questions that would assist me to more fully understand the effects of all of this trouble on your lives?"

Lucy and Tom gave me the go-ahead, and before long I was learning that this trouble had painted a highly negative picture of Lucy's identity as a mother, one that had made it very difficult for her to have connections with other mothers around the subject of parenting.

"What is it like for you that this trouble has so powerfully influenced your picture of yourself as a mother?" I asked Lucy. "How do you feel about the extent to which all this trouble has come between you and Daniel?"

In response, Lucy became quite tearful. I asked what the tears were all about, and Lucy began to tell me about her deep sadness over what she was missing out on as a mother and how she felt cheated by not knowing her son as she might.

Turning to Tom, I asked what he would say about the most significant effects of this trouble on his life. He was at first nonplussed by my question. He said that he hardly knew where to start. So I asked him about the ways in which this trouble had specifically affected his sense of being Daniel's father. He responded by saying that he had never been able to get onto the map in terms of being a father to Daniel—Daniel had never allowed him to assume such a place.

"Is this state of affairs okay with you, Tom?" I asked.

His response was part resignation and part despair: "Oh, I had my dreams, but what is the point?"

I was soon interviewing Tom about these dreams, which together we traced all the way back to the point of Daniel's conception. After a time, I asked, "So what would you say all of this trouble has done to those dreams?" His emotionally laden response was, "It has crushed them."

It was now time to turn to Daniel. "Would it be okay with you," I asked Tom and Lucy, "if I now consulted Daniel about the effects of all of this trouble on his life?"

"Go ahead," Lucy said, "but I doubt that you will get much out of him."

"Daniel," I said, "as you have heard, I've just been having a talk with your mom and dad about how all of this trouble has been affecting their lives. Now I would like to ask you some similar questions. Would that be okay?"

In response, Daniel shrugged his shoulders. I decided to proceed. "What has this trouble been talking you into about yourself? What sort of picture has it been painting of you?"

Daniel again shrugged his shoulders. I said, "Will it be okay if I assume that this shrug means that it's all right for me to proceed with my questions, and that you'll let me know if this isn't the case?"

I thought I detected a slight nod. Although I wasn't sure of this, I decided to proceed on the basis of this impression.

"Would it be okay by you if I asked your mom and dad for their thoughts on this?"

Another shrug.

"Thanks. I will assume that you are giving me the go-ahead, unless you tell me otherwise," I said with some enthusiasm, sensing a degree of collaboration from Daniel.

When I consulted Lucy and Tom about the question I had posed to Daniel, Lucy said she thought the trouble was painting a pretty dismal picture of who Daniel was. Tom elaborated on this, saying that he thought the trouble was talking Daniel into the idea that he was a "lazy good-for-nothing," a "waste of time as a person," and "even that he is useless." These descriptions were the very ones Tom and Lucy had been giving at the outset of our meeting, but they were no longer being collapsed onto Daniel's personhood. These descriptions had been deprived of their authority to characterize Daniel.

What a journey we had been on! At the outset of the interview Tom and Lucy had shared with me a number of highly negative identity conclusions that they and others had made about Daniel, and I had suspected that Daniel was secretly in agreement with this appraisal of who he was and of what his life was about. Now, thirty or forty minutes later in the conversation, we were experiencing the development of some shared sense that these conclusions didn't speak to the totality of who Daniel was, and that he also had an identity that was somehow separate from, and that even contradicted, these negative conclusions.

This opened the door for our work together to become more collaborative. "Daniel, what is it like for you to be talked into such negative things about yourself?"

This time, Daniel was shrugless in his response. He glanced at his parents, and, taking this as a cue, I asked them, "What

do you think it is like for Daniel to be talked into such nega-
tive ideas about who he is?"

In response, Tom said, "I guess that it makes him lonely—
and miserable too."

"I reckon that he is secretly sad about this," said Lucy,
"because I am sure that the wet patches that I sometimes see
on his pillow in the mornings are from tears."

I looked at Daniel, wondering whether or not he would
confirm this. Suddenly I saw a tear surfacing in the corner of
his eye. We all saw it. Daniel turned his head aside, his tear
evaporators working overtime. When he looked back, the tear
had vanished. But things were never the same after this tear. It
was a way forward. The existence of this tear was a signal that
Daniel had taken a position on the trouble that everyone else
had taken a position on. Now, for what seemed like the first
time, there was an opportunity for the members of this family
to be joined together, with me, in their efforts to break their
lives free from what had become such a terrible predicament.

This externalizing of "the trouble" was a starting point for
Daniel and his family. It was not the end of the process; it was
just the beginning. Once a name has been found for the problem, and once its tactics and effects are known, then there is
the chance for the person—and in this case the entire family—
to change their relationship with the problem.

Because naming the problem in an externalized way is such
an important step, let's consider it in more detail.

Naming the Problem

There are a number of ways to come up with an externalized name for the problem.

• Notice the adjectives that you are using to describe yourself, or that your friend is using to describe him- or herself, and turn them into nouns.

For instance, you can change "I am an anxious person" to "How long has *The Anxiety* been influencing you?" or "What does *The Anxiety* try to tell you about yourself?"

You can change "I feel really guilty about it" to "How is *The Guilt* getting in the way of what you want?"

You can change "He's always been a lot of trouble!" to "How has *The Trouble* gotten in the way of the connection you'd prefer with your son?"

• Sometimes it helps to personify problems.

For instance, when a young child wants to stop getting into so much trouble, you might inquire, "How does that Mr. Mischief manage to trick you?" "When is Mr. Mischief most likely to visit?" "How can we out-trick Mr. Mischief?"

• If it's hard for you to come up with a name that fits your problem, then you can initially refer to it simply as "The Problem" or "It." Over time, though, it can help to find a specific name, in your own words, that externalizes the problem.

Investigating the Influence and Operations of the Problem

The second step involves investigating the influence and operations of the problem. Once the problem is named in an externalizing way, then you can become an investigative journalist in your own life.

• How long has *The Anxiety* (or *The Depression* or *The Self-Hate* or *The Voice of Abuse*) been a resident in your life?

- When did _____ first come into your life?
- When is it most likely to visit? Does it come announced or unannounced?
- What are the "friends" of this problem? Does it work in tandem with other factors (like poverty, gender injustice, or racism)?
- What are the times and places where _____ is most powerful?

Exploring the Effects of the Problem

From an investigative journalist's position, you can also explore the effects of this problem.

- What are the effects of _____ at home, in the workplace, at school?
- What are the effects of _____ on your family relationships, your relationship with yourself, your friendships?
- What are the effects of _____ on your identity? What are its effects on your hopes, your dreams, your aspirations, your values? What is the problem talking you into about yourself?
- What are the effects of the problem on your future possibilities and life horizons?

Evaluating the Effects of the Problem

The third step involves working out what you think about the effects of this problem in your life.

- Are the effects of _____ in your life positive or negative? Or a bit of both?
- Do you want to change your relationship with this problem?
- Do you want to be completely free of this problem, or would you just like to lessen its influence in your life?

Asking Why

The fourth step of externalizing the problem involves working out *why* you want to change your relationship with the problem:

- Why do you want to change your relationship with this problem?
- What is this problem getting in the way of that you want more of in life?
- What would be different in your life if you could lessen the influence of this problem?

This is called taking a position on the problem, so that you know where you stand and you know where the problem stands.

A Note about Responsibility

While externalizing enables us to separate ourselves and our relationships from problems, it does not separate us from responsibility for the extent to which we participate in the survival of the problem. Let's look back at the story of Daniel. The trouble surrounding Daniel was having terrible effects not only on his life but also on the lives of his parents and many others. Externalizing this problem made it possible for Daniel to take a position in relation to the trouble for the first time. Externalizing the problem led Daniel to take *more* responsibility and increased his "response-ability"–he became more able to respond. Prior to this, Daniel had believed *he* was the problem. And if you believe you are the problem, all you can do is act against yourself. Put simply, externalizing problems can make it more possible for us to reduce the effects of the problem in our lives and in the lives of others.

It's Your Turn

Is there a problem influencing your life and identity at the moment? If so, you might like to take some time, either by yourself (with pen and paper) or with a friend, and go through the four stages of externalizing the problem. You can use the questions above to guide you. As you consider them, write down your responses. We will come back to these notes and use them later.

It often takes some time to work out a good externalized name for the problem. There are many options. What's important is that the name feels right to you. And it might not be the name you have been using up until now for the problem. For instance, if you currently call the problem you are dealing with "an anxiety disorder," it's not likely that this is a description that you came up with yourself, and therefore it is not likely to be the most fitting description. Other people who initially described their problem as an anxiety disorder have renamed it "The Fear That Comes" or "The Shakes" or "The Wobbles" or simply "The Anxiety." There's no "right" name, but it is important that whatever name you come up with for the problem enables you to see it and experience it as separate from yourself, not as a part of you or inside you. The person is not the problem; the problem is the problem.

Joanna's Sorrow and Fear[4]

When Joanna did this exercise, it took her a little while to find her preferred name for the problem she was facing. Others had told her that she had depression, and she thought this was probably true, but *depression* didn't seem to fully describe the tears that would stain her pillow when she woke, or the sense of fear that gripped her if she thought about going into public spaces. After considering the questions above, she decided that what was gripping her life was "The Sorrow and The Fear." This became her externalized name for the problem.

When Joanna considered the influence and operations of The Sorrow and The Fear, she realized these had come into her life about eighteen months before, when her mother had died, and shortly thereafter, when Joanna herself had been in a serious car accident. It seemed that the combination of these two events had provided an opportunity for The Sorrow and The Fear to become residents in her life. Joanna worked out that The Sorrow and The Fear seemed to work in tandem, and that they became worse any time someone was critical of her. This was when she would retreat from life, sometimes not leaving the house for several days. Some weeks, it was very hard for Joanna even to get out of bed.

In exploring the effects of the problem, Joanna realized that The Sorrow and The Fear had not only moved into her life, but also moved her out of her own life. She was no longer seeing the friends she used to see, she hadn't worked since the accident, and her sense of herself was changing. She was no longer looking forward to the future, and she was beginning to think she was a hopeless case.

Joanna evaluated the effects of The Fear as entirely negative in her life. It was The Fear that was undermining all her efforts to regain her equilibrium after the shocks of the previous year. It was The Fear that would prevent her from getting out of bed or leaving the house. She wanted The Fear gone so that she could once again be a bold woman in the world. When it came to The Sorrow, however, Joanna felt differently. There was a lot in this world to be sad about, she felt. Her favorite music had always been the blues. And if the tears she was crying at night were from dreams of her mother, whom she treasured, then these were tears of love. The Sorrow could stay, at least for a little while longer.

Changing Our Relationship with the Problem

After naming and taking a position in relation to the problem, it's time to decide how you wish to change your relationship with the problem. You may decide that you wish to:

- Walk out on the problem
- Eclipse the problem
- Dispel the problem
- Go on strike against the problem
- Set yourself apart from the problem
- Defy the problem's requirements
- Disempower the problem
- Reject the problem's influence
- Educate the problem
- Escape the problem or free your life of the problem
- Recover or reclaim the territory of your life from the problem
- Undermine the problem
- Reduce the influence of the problem
- Decline or refuse invitations to cooperate with the problem
- Depart the problem's sphere
- Redress the effects of the problem
- Come out of the shadow cast by the problem
- Disprove the problem's claims about your identity
- Reduce the problem's grip on your life
- Repossess your life from the problem
- Take your life out of the hands of the problem

- Resign from working for the problem
- Salvage your life from the problem
- Commence a comeback from the problem
- Steal your life back from the problem
- Tame the problem[5]

As you can see, there are many options. Please note, however, that it's often better not to "go to war" against a problem or "fight against" the problem. Sometimes this can make problems bigger, as they want to fight back! And unless we are trained fighters, we may actually have more skills in escaping, revising, negotiating, educating, taming, or organizing a truce with the problem than we do in fighting it. We need to play to our strengths. There are many ways we can change our relationships with problems and lessen their influence in our lives. Take some time to see if any of the options in the list above seem right for you.

Joanna decided she wanted to reclaim her life from The Fear and to become friends with The Sorrow rather than be overwhelmed by it.

Problems Can Be Persistent

It can be really difficult to change your relationship with a problem. It's not a matter of externalizing a problem and it will simply vanish. Problems can be slippery, and there are many different ways that we can seek to lessen their influence. For instance, once we have externalized the problem, we can use the written word to help us.

Joanna had always liked to write, and even when The Sorrow and The Fear were strong, she continued to write. Writing didn't involve having to talk with others, and Joanna was used to keeping a diary. With the help of her therapist, Joanna decided to use writing to assist her in reclaiming her life from The Fear and becoming friends with The Sorrow.

Joanna wrote two letters that proved particularly helpful. The first was addressed to The Fear:

To The Fear That Comes in the Mornings,

I am writing to you now to give you some advance notice. It's come to my attention that you have moved into my life. Somehow, without my noticing, you are here almost every day. This is a small apartment and there really isn't room for both of us.

I can imagine that you meant well on that day of the accident. I guess you were trying to warn me that my life was in danger, which it truly was. Well, thanks for this. But now, my life is not in danger and the ways in which you make me shake are not helping.

It's particularly unhelpful when you are here when I wake. When I feel you in my bones, it is very difficult to get out of bed and face the world. You can be overwhelming at times. I'm not sure if you know this.

It's been eighteen months now and I'm starting to claim my life back. My therapist tells me this might take some time. So don't panic. We're going to move slowly. This is just to give you some notice because you might want to find some other place to live.

Yours in determination,

Joanna

Joanna wrote the second letter to her niece, Felicity. Joanna had heard that Felicity, who was twelve years old, was also missing her grandmother (Joanna's mother).

Dear Felicity,

Your mom mentioned to me that you have been missing Grandma lately. Me too. I miss the sound of her voice and how she would always be there for me. Whatever was happening, I always knew she would be happy to hear from me. That's pretty special, isn't it? What do you miss? I know she loved you very, very much and that you made her happy, especially when you sang for her.

Sometimes, Felicity, I wake up and there are tears on my pillow. Does this ever happen to you? When I was your age, my mom (your grandma) would stroke my hair when I was in bed. I've been spending a lot of time in bed lately, and when I think of Grandma stroking my hair it makes me feel better. Is there anything that makes you feel better?

With love,

Aunt Joanna

Felicity wrote back to Joanna, saying that her letter had helped her remember that she used to sing to her grandma and that any time she started to feel sad, she was going to sing her grandma's favorite song.

Creating Our Own Documents

At this point, you might like to go back to the notes you took earlier in relation to:

- Naming the problem
- Investigating the influence and operations of the problem
- Exploring the effects of the problem
- Evaluating the effects of the problem
- Taking a position in relation to the problem

With these notes, you can now craft two letters:

1. A letter to the problem

Write a letter addressed to the problem. Within this letter, inform the problem that you have now learned its proper name and that you have uncovered some of the ways it works. Acknowledge some of the effects that the problem has been causing and politely let the problem know that things are going to change around here. There's no need to antagonize the problem, and this process may take some time, so we don't want to get ahead of ourselves. Simply write a short note to the problem acknowledging its existence and letting it know that change is coming and why this change is important.

2. A letter to someone else who may be facing a similar problem

Very often, the problems we are facing in life are also messing up other people's lives. Whether it's Mr. Mischief in a child's life, or The Anxiety, The Sorrow, The Self-Hate, The Voice of Abuse, or something else, these are problems that affect many people. At the same time, the way a problem operates in our lives will be different from the way it operates in any other person's life. This means that we have particular knowledge about the problem that nobody else has. This is called "insider knowledge." It is hard-won knowledge, and this makes it very valuable. Throughout the chapters of this book, the insider knowledge of people who have faced significant hardships and problems will be shared. At the same time, you will be invited to reflect upon and share your insider knowledge with others.

Take a pen and paper, or open a blank document on your computer, and start to write a letter addressed to somebody else who may be facing a problem similar to your own. Address the letter "Dear Friend," and try to catch them up on all you know about the externalized problem that you named earlier. Let them know the name you have given it and why. Tell them when this problem first came into your life, how it did so, its strategies and effects. Tell them what you think about the effects of this problem in your life and catch them up on your hopes for changing your relationship with this problem. Once you have finished the letter, print it out and put it in an envelope. You'll revisit this letter later.

Collective Conversations

Sometimes it's possible to have group conversations with an externalized problem.[6] These dialogues can even be quite amusing, particularly when the problem is personified and interviewed as if it were on *The Oprah Winfrey Show*. It can be freeing to finally bring a problem out of the shadows. This might be something you can do with friends or family members.

For instance, young people at Selwyn High School in New Zealand interviewed the "two faces of harassment" as part of their determination to reduce bullying, harassment, and discrimination in their school.[7] One young person played the interviewer while two other students played the roles of the two faces of harassment. They used this interview to externalize harassment and to let other students know about the Anti-Harassment Team of peer mediators they had established at the school. Here is just a short extract of the interview:

An Interview with Two Faces of Harassment

We would like to introduce to you now the reason why our Anti-Harassment Team exists. We would like to introduce to you two Faces of Harassment, who have very kindly agreed to be publicly interviewed, just this once.

Interviewer: Thank you for coming here today. Would you be able to tell us a little bit about where you come from?

Harassment 1: Well, I've been around since the dawning of time.

Harassment 2: Yes, well, I'm everywhere: families, community, institutions, workplaces, especially in schools.

Interviewer: So, if you've been around such a long time, you must be pretty successful. How do you account for your success?

Harassment 1: Well, I work on people's ignorance.

Harassment 2: Thrive on competition.

Harassment 1: We do really well where people care about being different. Schools are my playgrounds.

Harassment 2: Yeah. The teachers really help us. They label people as victims and bullies . . .

Harassment 1: . . and imply that the person is the problem. When people are labeled as victims and bullies and talked to individually, I can go right on in. That makes a perfect climate for me to get on with my dirty work and, well, people end up feeling as if it's them who's got the problem.

Interviewer: So, how about Selwyn College—have you been around Selwyn for a long time?

Harassment 1: Yeah, of course I have! Since the first day it opened.

Harassment 2: Just like any school.

Interviewer: What are your hopes for that school? What are your aims and ambitions?

Harassment 1: To make people's lives miserable—turn people against each other.

Harassment 2: To gain power by having people use me in dominating others and putting others down.

Harassment 1: Yeah. To be the main way that people relate to each other.

Interviewer: So how do you do that? How do you work?

Harassment 2: Well, we draw people into our way of working.

Harassment 1: Mmm, and become a habit. I've worked through generations and families, so I become taken for granted and people don't see me anymore.

Harassment 2: I make myself satisfying and enjoyable!

Harassment 1: Hmm. We become part of the accepted culture of how people relate to each other.

Harassment 2: Yeah. It comes back to the teachers, though. The best way has got to be through the teachers. They use their stand-over tactics in the classroom over the kids, and then the kids find their anger and use it on each other in the playground. It's great! They must make it hell for each other to learn.

Interviewer: So you seem pretty confident that you work well by yourselves, but who are your friends?

Harassment 1: Well, Gossip and Lies . . .

Harassment 2: Lies and Deceit . . .

Harassment 1: Yeah, and Resentment!

Harassment 2: Don't forget Jealousy.

Harassment 1: Greed, and Deceit . . .

Interviewer: What great company you keep! So, can anything stand in your way? You know, who are your enemies?

Harassment 2: We really don't have any . . .

Harassment 1: Well, there is something . . . I guess when I'm exposed and when I'm named.

Harassment 2: Yeah, I suppose that's true. When people see through my tactics and start realizing the effect that I've had on their lives, that can be a problem.

Harassment 1: Yeah, when people start to figure out my strategies and tactics.

Interviewer: So, how can people do that? How can people spot you?

Harassment 1: Well, I'm pretty tricky and I've got all sorts of disguises. I used to show myself in obvious bullying and streaks of violence, but one of my favorite tricks these days is when a group can be made to shut someone out by giving them the silent treatment.

Harassment 2: Yeah. We look for any way, any difference as a way of starting. Sexuality, race, appearance—you name it, it's a way to get started.

Interviewer: So, right now, how great is your hold on Selwyn College?

Harassment 2: Right now? Gee . . .

Interviewer: Do I detect that there might be some problems for you there?

Harassment 1: I've had a few difficulties at that school, because, well, the teachers there have these ideas, you know, about relating to students respectfully! And we had to work around this through other ways, through the students, because the staff had these weird ideas about cooperating together! I mean, that made everybody kind of really quite difficult. And then, a few years ago, they started this dreadful thing called the Anti-Harassment Team.

Harassment 2: Yeah, but at the beginning, you know, we didn't think it would be too much of a problem. They only had, what was it, about twenty kids and a couple of counselors and . . .

Harassment 1: Yeah, and we all know how easy it is to sneak around counselors!

Interviewer: So, what is it about this Anti-Harassment Team that's so bad for you?

Harassment 1: Well . . .

Harassment 2: Well, I just can't get in there!

Harassment 1: Yeah, they stick up posters and tell people about me, and people aren't even afraid to talk about me anymore. It's really bad! The worst thing is mediation. Yeah, they have this thing they call mediation and it's shocking!

Interviewer: So, this mediation sounds pretty bad. What happens in mediations? How come you walk away?

Harassment 1: Well, we just can't get it happening in there, you know. It doesn't help that the school thinks they're really important and lets students out of class to participate in them.

Harassment 2 [with disgust]: The teachers even respect them

The interview goes on to describe more about the initiatives of the students and the Anti-Harassment Team until the two faces of harassment start to feel a little bit hopeless:

Interviewer: It sounds like you want to give up on the whole school.

Harassment 1: Well . . .

Harassment 2: No, not at all! We're sticking around. We've still got a good chance.

Harassment 1: But it is unbelievable how hard it's getting . . .

Harassment 2: Yeah, but if we leave here, then we'll never be able to come back.

Harassment 1: It's hopeless here; we've got to put our energy elsewhere!

Harassment 2: But this thing's like a virus. If we don't stop it here . . .
Harassment 1: Look, do what you like, but I'm moving on.
Harassment 2: What? Are you going to wimp out on me again?
[They argue with each other, and then #1 walks out.]

These forms of group externalizing conversations, or narrative theater, in which problems are personified, are now being used in many contexts, including talking about Mr. and Mrs. AIDS in Southern Africa. Externalizing can be used in a wide range of ways, because it is not just a technique. Locating problems outside of people is a principle or a philosophy.

Our Influence on Problems

Earlier in this chapter we considered the influence that problems have on our lives. But it's not a one-way street. We can also have influence over the lives of problems. As we start to retell the stories of our lives and externalize the problems we are facing, we can begin to decrease the influence of the problem on us and increase our influence over the problem. There are many ways that we do this. The first is by exploring and honoring small moments in our lives when the effects of the problem are less present. These are called "unique outcomes," or sparkling moments.

Let's return to a question you considered earlier:

• What are the times and places where the problem is strongest? When and where does it have the most influence in your life?

Having thought about this again, now consider:

• What are the times and places where the problem is not as strong? When and where does it have less influence?

At these times and in these places, the problem may still be around, but clearly something is having an influence over it. Once again, taking an investigative journalist's stance, we can explore this unique outcome or sparkling moment. The following questions can assist. In that moment when the problem was less powerful:

- What was happening?
- Who was present?
- What were you and/or others doing?
- What were you thinking?
- Did you do any preparations leading up to this?

If our lives have been dominated by the problem for a long time, it can be hard at first to notice any of these sparkling moments. We may have to do some research.

Research

A simple way to conduct this research is to take a sheet of paper and draw a line down the middle. Over the following week, in the left-hand column, note any times and places where the problem was less strong. In the right-hand column, note who was present, what you and/or others were doing, and what you were thinking at the time. If you find it difficult to notice these times by yourself, perhaps you can enlist the help of a research assistant—someone who will point out to you times when you seem less dominated by the problem, if only for five minutes. You can also ask your research assistant to notice any actions you take during the week that are not in accord with what the problem would want. These can just be small steps.

For Joanna, for instance, remembering her mother stroking her hair was a unique outcome. Whenever she remembered this, it brought her some relief from The Sorrow and The Fear. Getting up each morning to feed her cat was a second unique outcome for Joanna. This act of care was not caused by The Sorrow or by The Fear, but was done out of Joanna's love. Even though sometimes it took all the energy she could muster, Joanna would get up every day and face the world in order to feed Lucky. Over time, as Joanna continued to recall her mother's touch, as she wrote a letter to notify The Fear of upcoming changes in their relationship, and as she shared insider knowledge with her niece Felicity, Joanna stopped seeing herself as a hopeless case and gradually started to say good-bye to The Fear. She and Lucky started to spend more time with each other during the day, and Felicity came to stay one weekend, which proved to be a turning point.

For Joanna, remembering her mother's touch and her relationship with Lucky helped to see her through the sorrowful and fearful times. No act or unique outcome is too small to include in your own research. Be on the lookout for any moments when your life is slightly less affected by the problem.

Special Skills in Getting through Hard Times

There is a second way that we can slowly start to free ourselves from the influence of problems. This involves starting to notice our special skills in getting through hard times. At first, these may be invisible to us, but everyone has ways of enduring hardship. This is true even in the hardest of contexts where you might at first think all is hopeless. For instance, colleagues in Rwanda who are survivors of the 1994 genocide have described to us some of what sustains them during times of hardship. The following extracts are from the document *Living in the Shadow of Genocide: How We Respond to Hard Times—Stories of Sustenance* (Denborough, Freedman, & White, 2008).

> *As we are living in the shadow of genocide, we have had to find ways to respond to great hardship. We have included here some of what gives us strength. We hope this document may be of assistance to others.*

Tears and Then Talking

Some of us are sustained by our tears. To cry, to shed tears, to allow them to fall, can make a difference. For some of us there is a tranquility that comes after tears that can allow us to sleep. After sleep, we may then take time to talk to someone. One person said,

> When I am sleeping, the tears that I have cried give me strength. When I sleep after I have cried, I am tranquil. There is no noise, only calmness. This way of sustenance came from my mother. Whenever my mother was in pain, she used to allow herself to cry. After her tears had fallen, she would go and talk to her friends.

Some of us are sustained by tears and then talking.

New Ways of Carrying On Traditions

There is a tradition in Rwanda that we respect the parents in our families. We see them as capable of everything, and we trust the answers that they give to us. We rely on their advice. Many of us lost our parents in the genocide, and so we have to find ways to continue to stay in touch with their advice. One person said, "When I have hard times, I write. I imagine that it is my father writing to me, giving me answers. I think these answers are the appropriate ones." Some of us are find-

ing new ways to carry on our tradition of seeking and respecting advice from our parents.

Your Own Special Skills

Depending on your context, your special skills in getting through hard times may be quite different from those of someone else. The following questions can assist you in coming to know your own skills. I will list them here and include the responses of Liz,[8] who attended one of our workshops.

• What is the name of a special skill, knowledge, or value that gets you or your friends and family through hard times?

  Liz: Tea and biscuits

• What is a story about this skill, knowledge, or value—a story about a time when it made a difference to you or to others?

  Liz: "Quite simply, there are times in life that call for tea and biscuits. At the first sign of trouble, some of us put the kettle on, whether we are cramming for exams, meeting others for study, or seeking comfort in times of shock. I broke my arm once when I was eight years old. The chair collapsed, and my mum immediately said, 'Let's make a cuppa and a plan.'"

• What is the history of this skill, knowledge, or value? How did you learn it? Whom did you learn it from?

  Liz: "There's something about a cup of tea that creates a space to breathe and think. We find comfort in warm tea and biscuits. I think this has been around in my life for as long as I have been alive. On the day I was born, I am sure my parents would have celebrated with a cup of tea."

• Is this skill or value connected in some way to broader traditions? Perhaps it originated in a cultural or community tradition or is tied to your family history. Are there proverbs, sayings, stories, songs, or images from your family, community, or culture with which your skills and knowledges are linked?

Liz: "Well, I'm English. I guess it's linked to this."

The group that Liz was taking part in as she answered these questions included participants from Hong Kong, China. When she said that she thought being English was the reason for her love of tea, they quickly reminded her that tea did not originate in England!

Many people have found it helpful to consider the special skills that get them through hard times and where these come from. These skills may include humor, remembering a loved one's touch, getting up to feed a pet, kindness, looking to the future, studying, being with someone else, spending time alone, walking, listening to music, singing, praying, telling yourself, "These times will pass," remembering those who are special to you, and so on. The special ways that we endure hardship are unlimited. Please note that they don't have to be anything out of the ordinary; tea and biscuits are not grand. If you have a number of different ways that you cope with hard times, and if some of these have both good and bad effects in your life (for instance, if alcohol helps you through hard times but also contributes to difficulties in your life), pick something uncomplicated for this exercise.

As you respond to the following questions, try to fill in as much detail as you can; paint a picture with words about your special skills in responding to hardship, and where these come from.

- What is the name of a special skill, knowledge, or value that gets you or you and your friends/family through hard times?

_____

_____

_____

- What is a story about this skill, knowledge, or value: a story about a time when this made a difference to you or to others?

_____

_____

_____

- What is the history of this skill, knowledge, or value: How did you learn this? Who did you learn it from?

_____

_____

_____

Is this skill or value connected in some way to broader traditions? Perhaps it originated in a cultural or community tradition or is tied to your family history. Are there proverbs, sayings, stories, songs, or images from your family, community, or culture with which your skills and knowledges are linked?

_____

_____

_____

Increasing our awareness of our special skills in dealing with hardship means these skills become more available to use in the future. Examining the histories of these skills where they originated and who we learned them from can also change how we understand ourselves, and the stories we tell about our lives.[9]

Looking Back, Looking Forward

This chapter has explored a number of significant topics. First, we considered ways to externalize problems. Ensuring that we don't see ourselves *as* the problem creates the possibility for us to change our relationship with the problem. This is a vital first step in rewriting the stories of our lives.

Second, we examined how sparkling moments—those times when the influence of problems is less strong—can offer us clues about how to weaken problems.

Third, we started to investigate the special skills that we have developed to navigate hard times. We also started to explore the histories of these skills. In doing so, we have started to transform the stories of our identity.

Reclaiming our lives from problems and rewriting the stories of our identity, however, can take time. This is particularly the case if the problems we are up against are influenced by violence, poverty, racism, sexism, and other forms of injustice. We will need to find the right audiences for our stories (see Chapter 3). We will need to consider matters of teamwork (see Chapter 4). And we will need to make preparations for our journey (see Chapter 5).

Notes

1. Michael White first introduced the concept of externalizing problems in his groundbreaking paper *Pseudo-encopresis* (1984). For more information about externalizing, see White, 2007.

2. The diagrams in this chapter were inspired by the work of Palestinian narrative therapists at the Treatment and Rehabilitation Center for Victims of Torture.

3. Some of the examples of externalized problems and questions in this chapter are informed by the work of Carolyn Markey and Chris Dolman, two narrative therapists at Dulwich Centre.

4. Joanna is a composite character.

5. This list is adapted from White, 2007.

6. The idea of collective externalizing conversations was developed by Yvonne Sliep and the CARE Counsellors of Malawi (Sliep & CARE Counsellors, 1996).

7. This work at Selwyn College was shaped by the two counselors at the school at the time, Aileen Cheshire and Dorothea Lewis. See Selwyn College, Lewis, & Cheshire, 1998, and Bruell, Gatward, & Salesa, 1999.

8. Liz is a pseudonym for a young woman who attended a training program with us at Dulwich Centre.

9. For more information about documenting skills in getting through hard times, see Denborough (2008).

CHAPTER 3

Finding the Right Audiences for Our Stories

THIS CHAPTER IS about finding an audience for our stories. It's also about *being* an audience or witness to the stories of others. We can make a big difference by how we witness and acknowledge the storylines of others, and other people can make a big difference in how we experience ourselves. In this chapter we will consider different sorts of audiences (real and imagined), various ways of acting as an acknowledging witness to the stories of others, and the use of documents, certificates, and rituals.

Imagined Audiences

You may be reading this book in a situation of profound isolation where it will be very difficult, if not impossible, to create a real audience for the preferred stories of your life. I used to work within prisons, so I am particularly thinking of those who spend twenty-three hours a day in a cell. And there are those who, for whatever reason, are living lives mostly alone in the community. Fortunately, even in contexts of profound isolation, it is possible to draw upon an imagined or remembered audience.

Who Would Be Least Surprised?

When we are trying to take positive steps in our lives or overcome a difficult problem, it can make a difference to hold in our minds someone who would be supportive of our efforts. Anyone. As you know, when I was thirteen, I wrote my first song. My first songs weren't good. In fact, they were pretty awful . . . and I couldn't really sing. I know this because I have recordings. When I hear those early songs, I think to myself, why on earth did I keep trying? Why wasn't I put off by the sound of my own voice? Well, I know why. It was because my father would sit in a chair in the adjacent room, and after every song he would call out, "Bravo!" This was to songs that must have sounded terrible! But still, always, I would hear "Bravo." I call this a "Bravo Voice." And I know how lucky I was to have it, and particularly how lucky I was to have a father who was supportive in this way. I have certainly met many people with fathers very different from my own.

The reason I mention all of this here is that, when we are trying to take new steps in our lives, or trying to overcome a problem, having a Bravo Voice to cheer us on can make a real difference. Perhaps the person who cheered for us was a family member, a teacher, a neighbor, a childhood friend, a religious figure. Sometimes the person won't be sitting in the next room. We might not see them anymore. They may no longer even be alive. But we can still imagine them and summon up their voice.

For instance, when Vanessa (Chapter 1) is struggling with the "good for nothing story," it can make a difference to summon up the voice of her sister, Salome, or imagine what her Nonna would say to her if she were still alive. Similarly, when Joanna (Chapter 2) remembers her mother stroking her hair, it lessens the power of The Fear and soothes her sorrow.

Being able to summon up or imagine the soothing voice of someone who cares for us can sometimes be life-saving. The following story is from a young man, Alex, who was in a profoundly difficult situation and yet found ways to survive. I met Alex when he was incarcerated for car theft and I was working in Long Bay Prison in Sydney.[1] Our meeting took place after he had been raped a number of times while in prison, and the story below describes not only the violence he experienced but also how he managed to survive it, what memories he held onto, and whose spirits he called on to get through the most anguishing times. Please note that in the first part of Alex's story, he describes the assaults he experienced.

It started when I went to court in the prison truck. There were eight of us in the truck. Four on each side. One of them started harassing me—he wanted my shoes. But when I gave them to him, he became very aggressive. I thought I had to do what they wanted me to do. I didn't want to get killed. They forced me. It was very painful. It was very distressing emotionally. I didn't want it to happen, but I couldn't really say no. There were three of them.

One was the main instigator. He just said to the others, "C'mon, have a bit of fun." How can one human being do this to another human being? Afterward I couldn't get to sleep at night. I got put on medication. Then I realized the medication made it worse. I was always thinking about it. I had bad dreams. Sometimes the inmates would talk about it: "You're good for this; you're good for that." One of the inmates that did it spread the word. It's a bit like a family tree. One person spreads it to two to four to eight. Half the jail knew. Some of the guys told me to stick close to them, that they'd help me out. I did that and they were helpful.

But then I was assaulted again, and then again. It's been very hard. I've cried myself to sleep and wanted to kill myself over it. I thought there must be something wrong with me if they wanted to do it to me. "Why aren't I strong? Why aren't I big? I wish I were tall." I felt so bad at times that it was either kill myself or survive. With what I've got outside now, I didn't want to ruin my life. If I had killed myself it would have been best for them. They would have thought, "Ha, he's killed himself just because of what we've done." They'd be boasting about it. I didn't want them to have that satisfaction.

When I asked Alex who would be least surprised at the strength he had shown, he spoke of his brother and his ex-girlfriend.

I think a lot of people I know outside would be very surprised at how strong I've been; they'd be wondering how I did it. I've tried to think about those people who care about me. My brother would be spinning out. He'd think, "My poor little brother." He's always cared for me, been there with me. When we were growing up, he was always pleased to see me, never too busy. Even if he had to go to work, he'd drive me there and I'd just sit there. One day he'll find out about this. It might be next week; it might be next year. It's hard for me to keep anything from him, so he'll find out one day. I used his spirit to get through all of this. If he were here we'd just talk about it.

It'd be very informal. He'd just be here, and hearing his voice would help a lot.

I think about my ex-girlfriend too. I'm writing to her now. Her spirit is already helping me to get through. I think of the things we've done together. She always talked me through situations. Even though she didn't speak much English, I learned Vietnamese. She'd say, "Just be strong, and I'll be with you all the way." When she'd get in trouble at school and she'd have to go to the principal, I'd go too. I'd say, "Anything you can say to her, you can say to me." I was really angry at him. I said, "It's as much my fault as hers." I guess there was some strength there. That's where I think I got some of it from. She'd be surprised at what has happened, but she wouldn't be surprised at my strength. It's gotten me through this far.

Thinking about his brother and ex-girlfriend made Alex realize that his recent "strength" has a longer history:

I guess I have a history of struggling against things. I'm adopted and I've had to deal with that. I've gotten in trouble before and dealt with that. Back then, there were times when I didn't have anyone to help me out and I had to do it all by myself. So I guess that history has made a difference. I try to think of the good things in life, what I've always done that made me happy: a TAFE [Technical and Further Education] course, my ex-girlfriend, family, brothers, sisters. I brought their spirits with me. I thought about what I was going to do when I got out of here. I talked to some inmates that I could trust. And I wrote letters to a lot of people. I didn't tell them what happened. I just said, "I'm feeling a little bit down emotionally; can you write to me and make me feel a little bit better?" On the inside, getting a letter is something big. I guess we just have to find our own ways to get through.

Three months ago I was going to kill myself, and instead of doing that I've come all this way. I hope this is of some help to others.

In the isolation of a maximum-security prison, Alex, after experiencing multiple assaults, found a form of comfort in an imagined audience of his brother and his ex-girlfriend. In thinking about them and what they would say to him, he realized the strength that he was showing had a long history.

At this point, you might like to think of one step that you have taken in the last few months to try to move your life forward. It doesn't have to be a big step, just something you have done to try to make a better life for yourself or for others.

- When you think about what it took to take this step, who in your past would be least surprised about this?
- What is it that they know about you, or that they may have witnessed you doing, that would have told them that taking this sort of step was important to you?
- What might they say to you to encourage you?
- In Alex's words, whose "spirits" could you bring with you as you take further steps?

Invisible Friends

There is another option for finding a supporting audience that might seem a little strange at first. It involves the possibility of relationships with invisible friends, as Michael White explains in an interview with Ken Stewart:

Michael: It is possible to work with people around the invention of an invisible friend, and at times it is even possible to resurrect people's relationships with invisible friends. Do you have any idea of how many children have friendships with invisible friends? . . . Just ask around. Ask children, or ask some of your adult relatives or friends about whether they had invisible friends in childhood. You will be surprised at the prevalence of these friendships. And do you have any idea of what a difference friendships with invisible friends make to children's lives?

Ken: It's not something that I think a whole lot about.

Michael: Neither did I, but some years ago, in response to a conversation with Cheryl White about invisible friends, I began to ask people questions about this. As Cheryl had predicted, I was surprised by the responses I received.

Ken: I guess that they provide support and reassurance, cure loneliness, and so on.

Michael: You can also pass the buck to them when things get tough. And invisible friends do more than all these things. They are very empathic and compassionate, and are prepared to go through all manner of experiences with children, even to join children in suffering. I am sure that you have heard of children getting a great deal of solace from being joined in illness by invisible friends. Invisible friends make it so much easier for children to take the things that they have to take. And children can tell invisible friends secrets, and, in so doing, give themselves a voice in this adult world where there is so little space given to children's voices.

Ken: I'm reminded of a popular comic strip here in the United States, Calvin and Hobbes, *about a boy, Calvin, who is about six or seven years old, and his stuffed tiger, Hobbes, who is quite animated and lively, and plays a significant part in Calvin's life . . .*

Michael: In this culture, at a certain point, children get talked out of their relationship with their invisible friends. This is considered to be developmentally appropriate. However, I do keep in mind that there are many cultures in which a person's relationship with the equivalent of invisible friends is preserved, and in which their ongoing contribution to the person's life is acknowledged.

In my work with people who are harassed by the voices of schizophrenia (or are having other very difficult experiences), I sometimes learn of a childhood relationship with an invisible friend. I can then ask these people questions about what these invisible friends meant to them, about how these invisible friends contributed to their lives in ways that were sustaining, about the circumstances of the loss of this relationship, and so on. I can ask people questions about what they think it was that they brought to the invisible friend's life, and to speculate about what the separation meant to the invisible friend. We can then explore the possibilities for reunion, and talk about how such a reunion might be empowering to both parties. And then we can put together plans for the reunion. I have attended many such reunions, and have found them to be very moving and warming occasions.[2]

If you had a relationship with an invisible friend in the past but somehow the two of you got disconnected, perhaps now would be a good time to arrange a reunion.

Being an "Acknowledging Witness" to Others

As well as evoking or finding a supportive audience for our own lives, we can be on the lookout for opportunities to be an audience to the lives of others. We can make a significant difference in how we witness the stories of others.

A *critical witness* can do profound damage if they side with the problem's view of a person. If a critical person sides with "The Voice of Abuse" or "Self-Hate," for instance, they can make The Voice of Abuse or Self-Hate so much more devastating in a person's life. If I had responded to Alex's story in a critical way, or if I had somehow gone along with the voice of the rapists by implying that there was "something wrong with him if they wanted to do it to him"–that is, if I had been a critical witness to Alex–I could have done him great harm.

On the other hand, an *acknowledging witness*[3] can make a huge contribution in enabling someone to restory their life. Being an acknowledging witness is different from simply offering praise or applause. While praise and applause (and "Bravo") have their place, sometimes they can inadvertently be experienced as patronizing, or as a judgment. Sometimes, too, it can be very hard for someone to hear and receive praise.

Let's imagine that Alex has just told his story to you. How could you be an acknowledging witness to him? First of all, you could practice what's called "double listening." You could listen to and acknowledge the two storylines in his words. There is a story of the injustice, the problem, the assaults that Alex was subjected to and the effects of this. That is one story. And then there is a second storyline of how Alex has responded, of his skills and his knowledge. To be an acknowledging witness involves acknowledging both of these storylines.

Here's an example of what you could say:

Alex, it sounds so unfair what you have been put through. Not only the rape by those three men, three against one, but then how people talked about it throughout the jail, how everybody knew. And it sounds terrifying that no matter where you turned you couldn't find safety, that you were assaulted two more times. It's so unfair that this made you think bad things about yourself . . . but you survived, Alex. There were so many things you did to find your own way to get through. I heard how you thought about your brother to get through and that you brought the spirits of your ex-girlfriend, your family, your brothers and sisters with you. And that you found some inmates you could trust. I heard that you also wrote to people on the outside to get them to write back to you, so you would receive their letters . . . what a great idea. And that you kept thinking about the good things in your life, so that you wouldn't give the rapists the satisfaction of knowing you harmed yourself. You found your own way to get through, Alex. It sounds like you know a lot about this, about getting through, about finding strength. Sounds like you have been finding strength for a long time.

There is one further step. At the end of Alex's story, he says, "I hope this is of some help to others." Often, when someone has been through a difficult experience, they end up isolated. They also end up hoping that what has happened to them hasn't been for nothing. An acknowledging witness can help someone like Alex to realize that what he has learned through these hardships can make a contribution to the lives of others. This will mean that Alex won't experience himself only as a victim, but also as someone with special knowledge. Hard-won knowledge.

Which *particular* aspect of how Alex responded to his situation were you most drawn to? Which aspect most captured your imagination, fired your curiosity, or provoked your fascination? Was there a particular skill or something Alex did that struck a chord for you?

Having thought about this, an acknowledging witness would then try to convey to Alex how hearing his story had somehow made a contribution to their own life. Has Alex's story moved you to think something, feel something, do something in your own life? I don't mean whether it simply moved you emotionally, but how did it move your thinking? How did it affect your understanding of your own life? What has Alex's story inspired or encouraged or challenged you to do?

Here are some of the ways that Alex's story has moved others to new thoughts, ideas, and actions. These are all "acknowledging witness" responses. I have highlighted the words that convey the difference Alex's words made in the lives of these witnesses:

- I loved the idea of writing letters to people–not telling them exactly what you have been through, but asking them to write back to you. This sounds like a letter writing campaign![4] **I am going to try this the next time I am struggling.**
- Your story has reminded me of an ex-girlfriend who was really significant in my life. After hearing that, Alex, I think **I'm going to write to her** just to tell her that I still think of her and remember what she meant to me. You don't often hear people remembering the good things that their exes did. It was good to hear that.
- I was adopted. I know what you mean when you say that it gave you strength. I don't often hear people say things like that. **It's made me think:** Has being adopted made me stronger?

If we, as acknowledging witnesses, let Alex know that as a result of his story we will now be taking different actions, that his words have made new things possible, then he will know that his story has been "of some help to others." He will know that what he has been through stands for something and that it means something important.

This is particularly relevant in relation to justice. There is no chance that Alex will achieve what is normally called "justice" in relation to the rapes he was subjected to. There is no chance that those people will be charged or sentenced. But there is more than one sort of justice. Being an acknowledging witness to someone is about "doing justice" to their stories. It is about acknowledging the injustice they have been through and acknowledging their skills, their knowledge, and, in the case of people like Alex, a storyline of "strength" that has been their response to the injustices.

Often, the difficulties people experience in life are due to injustices associated with class, race, gender, sexual identity, and so on. Being an acknowledging witness to others involves acknowledging these injustices and acknowledging the everyday small steps people are taking and the skills and strengths they are using in their lives.

Next time someone shares a story of their life with you, try to "double listen": Listen and acknowledge the hardship that they have endured and also how they have responded—the steps they have taken and the skills and knowledge they have demonstrated. And then try to convey how this person's story has led you to:

- develop a new perspective on your own life and identity, or
- reengage with neglected aspects of your own history, or
- make meanings of your own experiences that you have not previously understood, or
- initiate steps in your life that you have never considered, or

- think beyond what you routinely think, or challenge your-self to take some action to redress injustices.

The Written Word as Witness

Sometimes the written word can be a witness. The written word has power. It lasts. Often, unfortunately, it's used in negative ways. For instance, in psychiatric hospitals there are often huge files about the lives of patients. Sometimes every word in these huge files is negative and not one word has been written by the person. They are demeaning accounts of people's lives written by so-called "experts." When people with such huge case files came to see Michael White, he didn't read these files. He would say that he could learn what he needed to know much better by talking directly to the person concerned. He would, however, sometimes weigh these files. "Wow, that's a seven-pound file! What's it like lugging that around with you in life?"

The power of the written word can also be used for good. Throughout this book there are many examples of documents and letters, and you will be invited to write these for yourself and for others. Here we shall consider the possibility of making certificates.

Public Certificates

One way of sharing achievements with an audience is through the creation of certificates that can be shown to others. Jessie's story is a great example of this. It is told here by narrative therapist Sue Mann.[5]

Jessie and I have been meeting for about eight months, and recently she arrived in my office announcing that she was "not good" and that she had been having renewed panic attacks.

When I began to inquire about when this feeling of "not good" started, she told me a story.

Not long ago, Jessie had had a conversation with a friend who did not know of the sexual abuse that Jessie was subjected to as a child. In this conversation Jessie was telling her friend about the trouble she had been having with "nerves." Her friend unfortunately responded with, "You've just got to handle it . . . after all you have had a sheltered life because you've never worked [in the paid workforce]."

I was aghast and indicated so to Jessie, who went on to tell me that she felt very angry at her friend's remark. Her friend's comment had made Jessie wonder if she was "wasting her time," "putting it on," and having trouble with nerves just because she was "wanting attention."

But, unbeknownst to her friend, Jessie had been working. In the time that we had been meeting together, I had noticed just how hard Jessie was working. This was something that she had talked about herself. I found myself shocked at the realization that her efforts were probably invisible and unappreciated by many of her friends and possibly also her family. I wondered what it meant that our therapy sessions were probably one of the few places where she experienced acknowledgment for the effort and thoughtfulness she was putting into addressing the effects of the abuse. I wondered how a broader audience could be found for Jessie's work, knowledge, and skills.

I began by asking Jessie about the phrase "having a sheltered life" and what this evoked for her. Jessie spoke very eloquently about what it might have meant to live a sheltered life. She speculated that a sheltered life would have been one in which she was not abused. It would have meant having a childhood more like that of her own children—where they had her to watch over them. Jessie spoke about how she never had anyone else look after her children because she was determined to protect them. She spoke about how this had influenced her ideas about paid work.

Jessie also spoke about how having a sheltered life would have included having someone say to her (as she says to her grandchildren), "Never let anyone touch you on your private parts." Within a sheltered life she would have been believed when she told her mother and sister (twice) that the abuse was happening—as she would believe her grandchildren or children if they came to her.

We then spoke at length about the sort of work Jessie had been doing that might be invisible to others and listed off:

- Being available to her children
- Coming to counseling sessions
- Doing relaxation tapes twice a day
- Stopping herself from "having a go" at her partner
- Seeing her doctor and psychiatrist
- Not letting the panic attacks stop her from coming to our meetings
- Visiting friends
- Caring for her grandchildren

As we were talking, it occurred to me that if someone had been at college, they would not have worked harder or more determinedly than Jessie. I shared this with her. "In fact," I said, "if you'd been at college for the last six months, you'd probably have received a certificate by now!" I'm not really sure why I said this. Perhaps it was because my son was studying for exams at the time. Whatever the reason, the look on Jessie's face was one of amazement. "Would I?" she asked.

This response from Jessie encouraged me to suggest to her that perhaps we could make a certificate ourselves. Jessie embraced this idea with enthusiasm. Jessie had left school early with few reading and writing skills and had never received a certificate of any type. I invited her to consider what this award might acknowledge. She was very clear that it ought to acknowledge "how much I've been trying" and something about "fighting nerves." I agreed to have the certificate ready for her at our next session.

When I next saw Jessie, she was anticipating receiving the award. I showed her what had been written and asked her if she would like to sign it with me. "Read it to me first," she said. "That would be better."

And so I read out loud the words on the certificate:

This is to recognize the hard work done by Jessie in the fight against nerves. It is also to acknowledge the ways in which Jessie has worked hard throughout her life to stand up for herself in the face of difficult things and to look after those she loves.

Then we signed it.

The next time I met with Jessie, I wasn't surprised to hear that she had gone straight to the store to buy a frame and that the certificate was now hanging on the wall between her lounge and dining room. What did surprise me, but probably shouldn't have, was that Jessie had also shown the certificate to her children. "The kids are very proud of me," she said. Since we had last met, Jessie had also told two of her "very best friends" that she had been sexually abused as a child and that this was why she was having trouble with nerves. She had heard back from one of these friends that she was "like a big sister" to her. Jessie had also caught up with a friend from whom she had felt separated for a while. She heard from her that she thought Jessie "had done wonderfully." When I asked Jessie what it was like to hear these responses from her friends, she said, "I feel proud— I don't feel ashamed. It's not my fault."

In these ways, the certificate became a part of a broader public ritual of acknowledgment that involved the women and children who are significant to Jessie. Our therapy sessions are no longer the only place that Jessie's work to address the effects of sexual abuse is acknowledged. This now occurs in her relationships with her friends and every time someone notices the certificate hanging in her own home. In our future conversations together, I am looking forward to hearing more about other people in Jessie's past and present who would be acknowledging of what Jessie has achieved.

Certificates can also be made for children.[6]

Here is an example of a certificate for a child who has taken steps to overcome the problem that was leading him or her to regularly wet his or her pants. The child externalized this problem as "Sneaky Wee."[7]

Beating Sneaky Wee Certificate

This certificate is granted to _____
in recognition of his success at putting Sneaky Wee in its proper place.

_____ has turned the tables on Sneaky Wee. Sneaky Wee was running out on him. Now he has run

---

out on Sneaky Wee. Instead of soaking in Sneaky Wee, he is soaking in glory.

Awarded on the _____ day of _____

Signed _____
[therapist's signature]

And here is an example of a certificate for an adult:

Escape from Guilt Certificate

This certificate is awarded to _____
in recognition of her victory over guilt.

Now that guilt doesn't have such a big priority in her life, she is able to give herself priority in her own life. Now that she is not guilt's person, she is free to be her own person.

This certificate is to remind _____,
and others, that she has resigned from the position of super-responsibility in the lives of others, and that she is no longer vulnerable to invitations from others to live their life for them and to put her own life to one side.

Awarded on the _____ day of _____

Signed _____
[therapist's signature]

Creating a certificate

Do you know someone (adult or child) who has been taking steps to try to address a problem or hardship in their life? It could be an individual, a group, or even a family. If so, perhaps you can draft them a certificate. They don't need to have completely "solved" the problem to deserve a certificate. Like Jessie, this certificate could acknowledge the efforts they are making. Once you have created it, and depending on your relationship with the person, you may then ask them if they would like to receive it. If so, you could organize an award ceremony.

You may also wish to have a certificate created in relation to some aspect of your own life. You can design your own or find free templates online. Just search for *certificate template*, choose the design you would like, and draft the words you want to include. You can award it to yourself or ask a friend to do this for you.

Re-grading rituals

Many of us have to go through degrading rituals—rituals that make us feel unimportant, useless, or worse. Some of these degrading rituals happen regularly, like queuing up for food stamps or social security where workers appear indifferent to our lives or circumstances. And sometimes there are extreme rituals of degradation, such as sexual assault, being arrested, or being forcibly admitted to a psychiatric hospital. Whenever we have been through rituals of degradation, it can be significant to hold alternative rituals that are "re-grading"—rituals that honor survival and all that is important to us.

Included here are two stories of re-grading rituals. The first is from Jenny, a musician, theater director, meditator, and for a time in her life a woman who heard hostile voices (sometimes referred to as schizophrenia). Jenny was a member of Power to Our Journeys, a group of people who heard voices.

Together with supportive workers, they would sometimes gather for re-grading rituals:

> *Rituals have been a powerful part of building community and celebrating events for us. As a farewell to my life on workers' compensation, we had a ritual at a property just out of the city in the hills. Throughout the time I had been on workers' compensation, I had had a huge file. So we planted trees to replenish the earth for all the paper that had been used on my case. We also planted some trees for the koalas to replace the trees that had been wasted on all the paperwork. Then we had a bonfire and I burnt my rehab file! It was a great thing to do. We have lots of celebrations whenever we meet.*
>
> *It is important, I think, to create rituals that are full of love, that come from the heart and that lend support. These rituals are really important for me because they are a part of creating my new life in which there are happy times. We use rituals to mark the end of a horrible time and the beginning of hopefully a good time. To create meaningful rituals also means that everyone comes together; we get to see each other and share a warmhearted event. This Christmas, one of the project team members came and brought a parcel of sparklers and candles for each of us. On New Year's Eve, I lit one of the candles and one of the sparklers, you know, just on my own. Through ritual, we renew our strength and build on friendships.*[8]

One of the most significant stories about re-grading rituals that I have ever heard comes from a young woman named Kate. When Kate was seventeen, she was raped in a violent attack by a stranger; there was a weapon involved. She was walking along a beach in daylight on a holiday with her family. But this was not the end of Kate's story. She survived the attack, and having been through a profoundly traumatic and degrading ritual, Kate and those who cared about her took steps to reclaim her life. Here is an extract of her story in her own words:

A Story of Survival

Sharing the Story

I knew right from the beginning that I didn't want this to be a secret. My parents told my brother when we finally got home that night at 2:30 a.m. The next morning, I remember, my grandmother came over and gave me a hug. That's when I started crying. I think I was lucky that I felt I had friends I could tell. I wasn't a thirteen-year-old who hated herself and didn't live with her parents and therefore felt like she had no one to tell. And I didn't have a wild reputation that might have meant people wouldn't believe me. You often hear of children who've been sexually abused telling their parents or somebody and the person refusing to believe it. I never had any of that. That would be so hard to deal with.

Telling people wasn't as easy as I thought, because once I'd told people, or my mom had called various members of my family, then when I saw the people who had been told they didn't say anything to me. That was pretty hard to deal with. I guess they felt that maybe I didn't want to talk about it.

But I kept telling people. Andy, my boyfriend at the time, was great. Andy was the person who listened to it all. I didn't have to protect him. I just told him how it was. A week later, I told all my close friends that I'd been raped. They were all shocked and upset and started crying. Initially this was fine, but then over time no one knew what to say, and I got really upset and angry. I thought, "Look, these are my best friends; why aren't they saying anything to me?" So I dragged them along to counseling with me. That was really good. My counselor asked a few questions, and it was so much easier to talk as a group. I think my friends just didn't know what to say. Some really nice things came out of the conversation in the counseling. One friend said, "I wish it had happened to me instead of you." At the time I thought this was really touching. Later on I found out that she'd been raped by her father when she was ten years old. I couldn't believe it then, that this had happened to her before, and yet she still said that she wished it upon herself before me. I was really touched by that. I was the first person she had told. In some ways, having it happen to me and my talking about it gave her the strength to tell her friends for the first time.

Reclaiming the Night

We were so young. Maybe at the time I might have felt that some of my friends could have done a better job, but we were only seventeen. And with my girlfriends I think it was too close to home. We never thought this could happen, and when it did I think it opened the possibility in my girlfriends' minds that it could happen to them, too. It made it so hard to talk. We were so close that it was just unbearable for it to have happened. They didn't want to think about it too much; it was too painful.

Sometimes if we couldn't find ways to talk about it, it was better to do something together. When "Reclaim the Night" [an annual feminist march] came around, it seemed like the perfect opportunity. I felt like we should all go together. We do lots of things as a group, and I thought it was really important that we do this together, because then they'd feel like it was a good way for them to help me without having to say anything. Nearly all of my friends went. It was really good. Christine, Andy's mom, came too. It was just great to be out there walking and making a difference, with people honking their horns and clapping in support. It was a really good way to bring my friends together. At the end of the night I called my mom and asked her to pick me up because I didn't want to catch the bus home in the dark. I guess it was taking care, but it felt kind of strange, too. That night meant a lot to me.

Marking the Anniversary of Survival

By the time the one-year anniversary of the rape was coming up, I felt I had to do something to mark the occasion. To say, "Look, I'm still here. I haven't forgotten about it, and it's just not going to go away. But I have survived." The dominant way of viewing rape is to see the woman as a victim who feels ashamed and that she's got to forget about the rape, to get over the story of humiliation and shame, to bury it, to get back to normal. Whereas, if you believe in telling a story of survival, then it's always progressing and ongoing. You're not going to forget, but you're going to be moving along. So on the anniversary of the rape I asked my friends out to dinner. When I first suggested this, I was nervous, and I think the way that I invited people confused them a bit. I kind of announced it by saying, "You know, the fifteenth of January—

that's my one-year anniversary. I thought we could go out to dinner to celebrate." And my friends thought, "What? Celebrate that you got raped?" And then I could explain: "No, to celebrate that I've survived." I don't think we're used to talking about survival, and so it can be confusing at times. Pretty quickly they understood that to stay home that night and watch videos would have been conforming to the victim role. It would have been staying inside away from the street, mourning what happened rather than going outside and being a part of life and saying, "I'm still here." So we went out to dinner together.

After we'd eaten, Andy read out a speech that talked about the importance of friendship. He spoke of my courage, too, but mostly we wanted to stress how friendship had so much helped the process of survival. One of the guys there then said that he thought I was one of the strongest women that he knew and how all of this had changed his attitudes toward a lot of things. He spoke about how any tolerance he had once had for sexist jokes and all that kind of stuff had now completely gone. He said that once he may have half laughed and just let it go, but now he wouldn't stand for it. He wouldn't tolerate it at all. I was really glad that he could say that. Another friend, who didn't come to the march, said something really helpful. I had been going on about how Davo [this was the name Kate had given to the rapist] had gotten away with it, and she said that she hadn't spent any time thinking about Davo, that she didn't see the point. She said, "I haven't thought about him at all, because that's not important to me. It's you that's important to me. How you're coping. He doesn't deserve any of our attention in any way." It helped a lot. It made me think about one of the women in my counseling group. When the guy who had raped her was being sentenced, we stood outside the court and she just read her poetry—poems of her survival. There was a group of people, and the media was there. She was determined to take the attention away from the perpetrator. There's always so much attention on him. She wanted to focus some attention on the survivors and the stories of survival. That felt really good.

Another one of my friends, Fiona, who is really quiet and didn't say anything at the dinner, came up to me later. She said, "I'm not religious, but I've been praying for you and thinking about you." Fiona never says very much; she keeps to herself. When she does say something, it's worth listening to. Paul, another friend, came up to me some time later and apologized for not being more of a support. He said, "I'm sorry, but I've had a rough year myself. I just told my parents I was gay, so I've been kind of dealing with that." Somehow we have all built up the trust between us. These friendships are very special to me. We have shared such rich histories. They are so much a part of my story of survival.

Creating Our Own Rituals

If we know someone who has survived a difficult time, like Kate, or someone who is moving through a transition, like Jenny saying good-bye to her life on workers' compensation, perhaps we can play a part in developing a ritual with them. These are re-grading rituals that honor people's skills, knowledge, and survival.

Alternatively, we can plan rituals for our own lives. We can choose the most appropriate place, the music we will play, the people and pets we may invite. We can think about whether there are any people who are no longer alive whose memory we would like to evoke in this ritual. Perhaps there is a document, letter, or certificate that could be awarded.

Looking Back, Looking Forward

In this chapter, we have considered finding an audience for our stories and *being* an audience or witness to the stories of others. We have also explored the use of documents, certificates, and rituals. With our certificates in hand and our rituals in place, let's turn to considerations of teamwork.

Notes

1. Alex's story appears in the Prisoner Rape Support Package (Denborough & Preventing Prisoner Rape Project, 2005).
2. The interview between Ken Stewart and Michael White first appeared in White, 1995b.
3. In narrative therapy, Michael White refers to acknowledging witness responses as "outsider witness responses" (White, 2007).
4. Stephen Madigan has described letter writing campaigns (Madigan, 2011).
5. Sue Mann's writings first appeared in Mann, 2000.
6. In fact, it was children who first taught narrative therapists about the importance of the audience, as Michael White (2007) explains:

In the 1980s, along with my friend and colleague David Epston, I began to actively engage audiences in my work with families. This was partly inspired by our observations of the extent to which many of the children we met with spontaneously recruited audiences to the preferred developments of their lives. For example, in the context of our meetings with families, children would be awarded certificates that acknowledged significant achievements in their effort to reclaim their lives from troublesome problems. Invariably these children would show this certificate to others—perhaps to their siblings, cousins, friends, or peers at school. This usually had the effect of prompting questions from the "audience," which provided an opportunity for these children to give an account of the feats signified by the certificate and at times to actually demonstrate their prowess. These questions and responses from the "audience" were clearly influential in acknowledging the preferred developments in these children's lives, in contributing to the endurance of these developments, and in extending them. (p. 178)

7. The certificates in this chapter are based on examples from White and Epston, 1990. Children in Australia refer to "wee" where in the US they might say "pee"!

8. The story of Jenny's ritual with the Power to Our Journeys group was first published in Brigitte, Sue, Mem, and Veronika, 1997.

CHAPTER 4

Teamwork: Remembering Who Is Important to Us

THERE ARE MANY different ways of thinking about our lives and our identities. One way is to think of our life as a club, an association, or a team. This metaphor makes it possible for us to consider, who are the members of our club of life? These "members" can be alive or no longer alive. They may be people we see regularly, or pets, or people and heroes whom we hold in our memories and our minds.

In this chapter, we will consider who we would name as the "members" of our team. In the process, we may choose to place more emphasis on some memberships and less on others. We can also then take a team approach to addressing problems and seeking our goals.

Making deliberate decisions as to whom we wish to include in our "team of life" involves a special sort of recollection called "re-membering." It was first described by anthropologist Barbara Myerhoff (1982):

> To signify this special type of recollection, the term *re-membering* may be used, calling attention to the re-aggregation of members, the figures who belong to one's life story... (p. 111)

The best way to explain this is through the following story. When Louise consulted Michael White, they had conversations about whom she wished to consider the key "members" of her life and identity. Along the way, she decided to hold a re-membering ritual.[1]

Louise sought consultation in the hope of dealing with some of the "remnants" of the abuses that she had been subjected to by her father and by a neighbor (a man who lived two houses away from her family home) during her childhood and adolescence. Over more than a decade, she had taken many steps to reclaim her life from the effects of these abuses. The two therapists she had consulted during this period had been very helpful to her in this project, and life was now going quite well for her. However, there were still occasions when Louise found herself entertaining negative thoughts about her identity, and these thoughts would recruit her into self-accusation. Although she had developed ways of shaking off these negative thoughts and of freeing herself from self-accusations, and although she knew these negative thoughts and self-accusations would not prevent her from having a good life, Louise hoped that further steps could be taken to eradicate these experiences from her life.

When I consulted with Louise about her experiences of these thoughts and self-accusations, she said that at times it was almost as if she could still hear in them the voices of her father and her former neighbor. Apart from the way that these voices were linked to the negative thoughts and self-accusations, Louise said that their presence made it difficult for her to be open to the positive things that others had to say about her identity. I asked Louise to check my under-standing of her concerns: "Is it that your father and this neighbor claimed a privileged say in matters that relate to your identity, and that, because of the steps that you have taken to reclaim your life from the abuses, you are now vul-nerable to these claims only at times when you find yourself in stressful circumstances?"

"Yes, this is a good understanding," came the response.

"And is it that you would like to take steps that would dis-possess your father and this neighbor of any say whatsoever at these times?"

Louise again responded in the affirmative.

At this point in our conversation, I was thinking of the life-as-a-club metaphor. So I asked Louise if, in thinking about her life as a club with members, it would fit for me to speak of her father and the neighbor as having claimed an elevated membership status in her life.

"This makes sense," said Louise.

"In that case, perhaps a re-membering ritual might be help-ful." I then began an explanation. "Have you ever been a mem-ber of any club that had a constitution or charter?" I asked.

"I was a member of a tennis club when I was nineteen," replied Louise.

"Would it be possible for you to obtain a copy of the consti-tution of this club?"

Louise said that she could try, but didn't know if the club still existed. "Why do you want these documents?" she asked.

I explained that these documents might provide a basis for the structuring of a re-membering ritual, in which the mem-berships of her father and the neighbor could be downgraded or revoked, and in which some of the other memberships of her life could be upgraded and honored. "Perhaps, through such a ritual, you might find yourself having a lot more to say about which of the members of your life are granted some authority on matters of your identity." I then explained the proposal for a re-membering ritual, and Louise said that she was enthusiastic to give it a try.

Louise brought to our next meeting a constitution on which she had already highlighted the sections relevant to the suspension, the revocation, and the honoring of memberships. We read together the relevant clauses and began the task of translating them into documents that would become part of a ritual that would provide Louise with an opportunity for the revision of the status of the membership of her life. Louise had made a decision to expel the neighbor from her club of life, but not her father. Rather, it was her intention to very significantly downgrade his membership so that his voice on matters of her identity would cease to have a hearing.

Louise's translations of the relevant clauses were quite formal:

You are hereby given notice of the following charges (see below) in regard to actions that are in contravention of the regulations governing membership of Louise's club of life. These charges will be heard by the ethics committee on September 7th. You are advised that you have the option of making submissions regarding these charges. The deadline for any such submissions is September 1st. These submissions must be tendered in triplicate, and via registered mail.

Without prejudice,

Louise, Chief Executive Officer

Louise had also reached decisions about which memberships of her life were to be upgraded: that of a friend, Pat; her Aunt Helen; one of the counselors, Jane, who had been so helpful in assisting her to reclaim her life from the effects of the abuse; and a psychiatric nurse, Pauline, who had stood with her through some particularly difficult times.

The very writing of the notices to her father and the neighbor had a powerfully invigorating effect on Louise. She deliberated as to whether or not to mail these notices, along with the lists of charges. Ultimately, she chose not to do so. We then moved on to the preparation of the notices that were to go to Pat, Helen, Jane, and Pauline. These notices advised these women that, on account of their contributions to challenging the voices of abuse in Louise's life, they were to be granted honorary life membership in her club of life. Before mailing these notices, Louise would call these women to provide some background, and would ask them if they, as members of her "ethics committee," would be willing to join in a ritual ceremony in which the charges against her father and her neighbor would be read. She would also ask these women if it would be acceptable to them if the contributions they had made to being an antidote to the voices of abuse in her life were honored in this ceremony, and if they would join her in a celebration afterward.

Louise received a positive response from all of the women, and three weeks later we assembled for the re-membering ritual. In the first part of this ritual, Louise, with the assistance of some questions from me, made known the purposes of the ceremony and of her determination to dismantle the authority of her father and neighbor in all matters that related to her life.

Louise then read aloud the charges and asked that the ethics committee join her in reaching a decision on these. It *was confirmed that Louise's father and the neighbor had breached many of the membership regulations of Louise's club of life. A unanimous decision was made to expel the neighbor from Louise's club of life and to downgrade her father's membership to that of an associate with provisional status.*

Louise then spoke of the significant contributions that those present had made in assisting her to reclaim her life from the effects of the abuses that she had been subject to. She acknowledged the extent to which the voices of Pat, Helen, Jane, and Pauline had challenged the authority of the voices of abuse in her life. These women were then invited to engage in a retelling of what they had heard. In this retelling, they responded to some questions: "How have you been able to join with Louise in this way?" "What is it that has you acting against these injustices?" "What is it like for you to know that Louise has included you in her life in this way?" "What does it mean to you that the voices of abuse haven't been able to silence your voices?"

In their responses, Pat, Helen, Jane, and Pauline shared stories from their own lives that had linked them to Louise's, and these spoke of shared values, concerns, and themes. For example, Jane spoke of her parents' contribution to her own consciousness of injustice, and of the part that this had played in her joining Louise in her project of reclaiming her life from the effects of the abuses she had been subjected to. Louise spoke of what it meant to her to be connected to the lives of these women in this way, and offered to them life memberships of her club of life. These life memberships were readily accepted. We then moved on to the celebratory part of the ritual.

This ritual had a powerful effect on Louise's experiences of the voices of abuse. From this time on, under circumstances of stress, these voices were never more than a whisper–and at these times they were quickly dispelled by the voices of those who were life members of her club of life. And there were other developments that were a direct outcome of the re-membering ritual. For example, Louise developed a connection with Jane's parents and began to take steps to reclaim her relationship with her mother.

Your Life as an Association or Club

If you were to think of your life as an association with members, what would its constitution be? Who would its members be? Draw up a list of people, pets, heroes, imaginary friends, sporting teams, religious figures, and so forth whom you would include as part of your "club of life." If there is anyone to whom you would give a particular award or lifetime membership, indicate this in some way. Alternatively, if there is anyone who currently has a suspended or downgraded membership, indicate this in some way, including the steps they will need to take to have their full membership reinstated (if this is possible).

A Sporting Metaphor

For those of us who enjoy sports, it can also be helpful to think about our life as if it were a sporting team. I learned the significance of this from young men who had been through wars. A few years back, I was part of a team invited to develop ways of working with former child soldiers. When we visited Uganda, I learned of the importance of "football" (soccer) in so many young men's lives. Let me paint you a picture of our visit to a refugee camp:

Picture this. We are close to the Sudanese border. It's a hot morning, and our hosts have generously driven us closer to the border of Sudan so that we can meet with a group of young men. These young men are refugees and former child soldiers. When we arrive, they are on the football field. There are yelps of delight coming from their direction. As we approach, we see skillful moves—a dance, almost—being instantly orchestrated by up to twenty-five participants. There seem to be many aims of the game, and scoring goals appears to be only one of them. At regular intervals, someone takes a few moments to balance the ball in gravity-defying ways on one foot, or on his head. Teammates create regular opportunities for celebration, for laughter, for camaraderie. These young men are performing artistry with their bodies. Despite the troubling memories they carry with them, they are joined in joy and delight. Can we build upon this? Can our approaches in responding to trauma build on the skills and knowledge young people display on the football field?

Inspired by these young men and by re-membering practices, we started to use what I call the "Team of Life" approach.[2] It's another way of thinking about our lives. Anyone can use the Team of Life approach, although it helps if you know a bit about a team sport. If you don't follow any sports, perhaps there is a young person in your life who does and who might like to do this exercise with you. You could ask them to assist you to do the process first, and then they might be interested in doing it themselves.

The first step involves drawing up your "team sheet." Everyone's team sheet looks different; there's no right or wrong way to do it. And you can use any team sport as its basis. Figure 4.1 shows an Arabic team sheet from Salma, a Palestinian woman who loves football.[3]

Dwayne, on the other hand, is a gridiron fan. Here's his description of who he chose to include in his Team of Life:[4]

My "safety," who looks out for me and guards my team, is my mom.

Figure 4.1. A Palestinian team sheet, facilitated by narrative therapist Nihaya Abu-Rayyan.

My "defense," who protects my dreams and what is important to me, is my grandfather.

My "offense," who encourages me to score and achieve in life, is my mom.

My "coach," whom I have learned the most from, is my god-brother. Some of the things he has taught me include how to be patient, how to "act my age and not my shoe size," and to never give up.

My "substitutes," the people who are sometimes on my team and other times are not, are my uncles.

My "home territory," the place I feel most at home, is my bedroom.

The spectators, fans, and supporters in the stands are my friends and family.

My team sponsor is Nike.

And our team motto is "Get with it!"

Julie-Anne, who lives in New York, likes basketball. Regarding her Team of Life, she says, "I play offense, my little sister defense, my big sister guard, my stepdad center, and my mom coach."[5]

Creating Your Own Team Sheet

The following questions can be used to assist you in creating your own Team of Life. They may be altered slightly depending on what sport you use as the basis.

Part One: Creating Your Team Sheet

Goal Keeper, Safety, Center

• If you had to name who is most reliable, who looks out for you and guards your goals, who would this be? This could be a person, a group, even an organization.

Defense

• Who else assists you in protecting your dreams? In protecting what is precious to you?

Coach

• Who is it you have learned the most from in life? It is possible to have more than one coach. And it's possible that they may or may not still be alive. What are some of the things that they have taught you?

Your Offense

• Who assists you and encourages you in trying to score?

Other Teammates

• Who are some of the other teammates in your life? Those you play with? Those whose company you enjoy?

Your Position

• What is your position on this team? Where would you place yourself?

Substitutes

• Are there people who are sometimes on your team and sometimes not? People who are very helpful to you in life some days and then on other days not helpful at all? At what times do they help? At what times do they not help? How have you learned the difference?

Spectators, Fans, Supporters in the Stands

• When you are at your home ground, who are the supporters you imagine in the stands? Who are the people (living or nonliving) who are hoping you will do well?

Key Values You Are Defending

• What are some of the important values of your team? What is this team standing for? What values are you defending? (Put these behind your goals.) What is the history of these? Have they been a part of your team for a long time?

Home Court/Field

• What is your home ground? Where are the places you feel most at home? You may have more than one place. They may even be in more than one country. Your home ground may be somewhere that you go regularly, or it may be somewhere that you visit only in your memories or dreams now.

Team Song

• Do you have a particular song that means a lot to you? That you could call the "theme song" of your life at the moment? If so, what would it be? Why is it significant to you?

First-Aid Kit

• When your team faces a difficulty (an injury, a player going down), what do you turn to? What supports your team in hard times? What is in your first-aid kit?

Other Themes

• What is your team emblem?
• What is your team motto?
• Who is your team mascot?
• Who is your team sponsor?
• Who is your team manager?

Team sheets don't always have a lot of people; they name only those who are significant to us. Figure 4.2 is a team sheet from Tony, a young man who came to Australia as an unaccompanied refugee.[6] He named "Mum" and "God" as his goalkeepers.

What seemed most significant was when Tony tried to name what his team stood for, what it was defending. He took this question very seriously. He was quiet for some time, then said, "It doesn't matter if you lose, as long you try your best." This

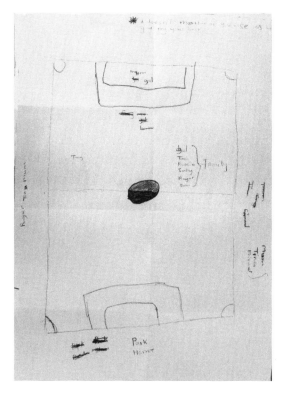

Figure 4.2. Tony's team sheet.

was the guiding philosophy of Tony's team. When I asked him if he would write this along the top of his team sheet, I saw him hesitate. Writing in English was a great challenge, so I sat with him and ensured that this act of writing was not a solitary one. We were in it together. Occasionally he would ask for clarification. The process was a long one; it probably took close to ten minutes for Tony to write out his team's philosophy. When he completed it, I felt like cheering.

If you choose to try this with a young person or by yourself, try to think widely. Those you include on your team sheet do not have to be people you see regularly. They may no longer be alive. You may choose to include figures from your religion or from your past. Pets have sometimes been included, too.

Part Two: Creating a Goal Map

The next step in the process involves identifying one collective goal or achievement that this team has *already* scored. If you are undertaking this process with a young person, it's really important that you don't ask what goal they have *individually* achieved. That would be quite a difficult question, and it leaves much more room for failure. Instead, we are seeking to acknowledge a collective goal. Perhaps the young person may have only played a very small role in the achievement of this goal. In no way does that diminish the significance of the team's achievement. We are actually more interested in reflected glory than individual glory in the Team of Life process!

This is the same if you are doing the process in relation to your own life. Consider one "goal" that *the team* has already scored. Examples include "staying together through hard times," "making a new friend," "making it through a hard year," "finishing high school," and "becoming a nice boy again."

Having thought of the past goal that has been achieved, we draw it!

- Draw a goal map that indicates the different contributions that people made to the achievement of this goal. Can you describe who was involved in the "scoring" (attaining) of this goal? Was it a solo effort, or did other members of your team of life help out? How? Did your coach encourage you or help you with tactics?
- What parts did everyone play in this? Go through each theme (home ground, goalkeeper, defense, attack, team-mates, etc.).
- What skills, knowledge, values did you or others use in the scoring of this goal?
- Where did these skills/knowledge/values come from?
- What training did you and others do to make it possible to score this goal? How often did you do it? Each day, once a

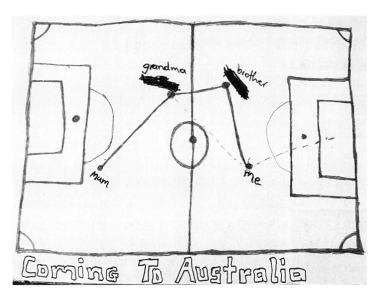

Figure 4.3. A goal map: Coming to Australia.

week? Where did you train? How did you learn how to do this training? Did anyone show you how?
• Draw a scoreboard on one corner of the document and mark this goal!

Figure 4.3 shows a goal map created by another young person who came to Australia as a refugee.

Figure 4.4 demonstrates how Tony (whom I mentioned above), his sister, his mother, a relative, and a friend acted collectively to "stay together through hard times." I discovered that one of the people listed on this goal map had passed away, but Tony continues to honor their contribution.

Part Three: Celebrating the Goal

Celebration is a profoundly significant aspect of sporting culture. Within team sports, these are collective celebrations of collective goals. It doesn't matter which member of the team scores; everyone celebrates. In life in general, however, so many significant achievements against the odds are never acknowledged, let alone celebrated. Therefore, in the Team of Life, once we have created a goal map of a previous accomplishment, we talk about the different forms of goal celebrations that take place in sports.

Figure 4.5 is a list of goal celebrations compiled by young refugees to Australia who know a lot about soccer. Which of these would be most appropriate to use to celebrate your goal? Or are there other forms of celebration you would prefer? Ideally, celebration is social; so, if you are sharing this process with a young person, you might also consider the appropriate venue for celebrating this goal. Who should be there? What music should be playing?

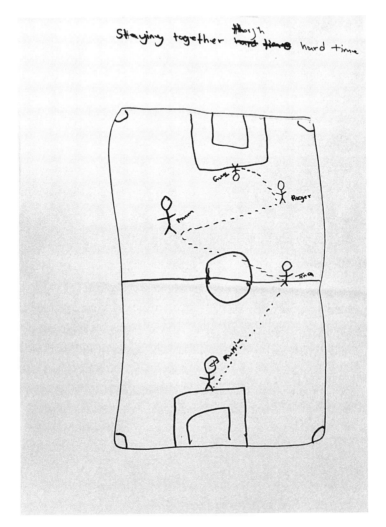

Figure 4.4. A goal map: Staying together through hard times

Speaking of music, at these goal celebrations we sometimes play the "theme song" of people's teams. Sometimes people even write their own theme songs. Tony, for instance, wrote the following lyrics to represent his team:

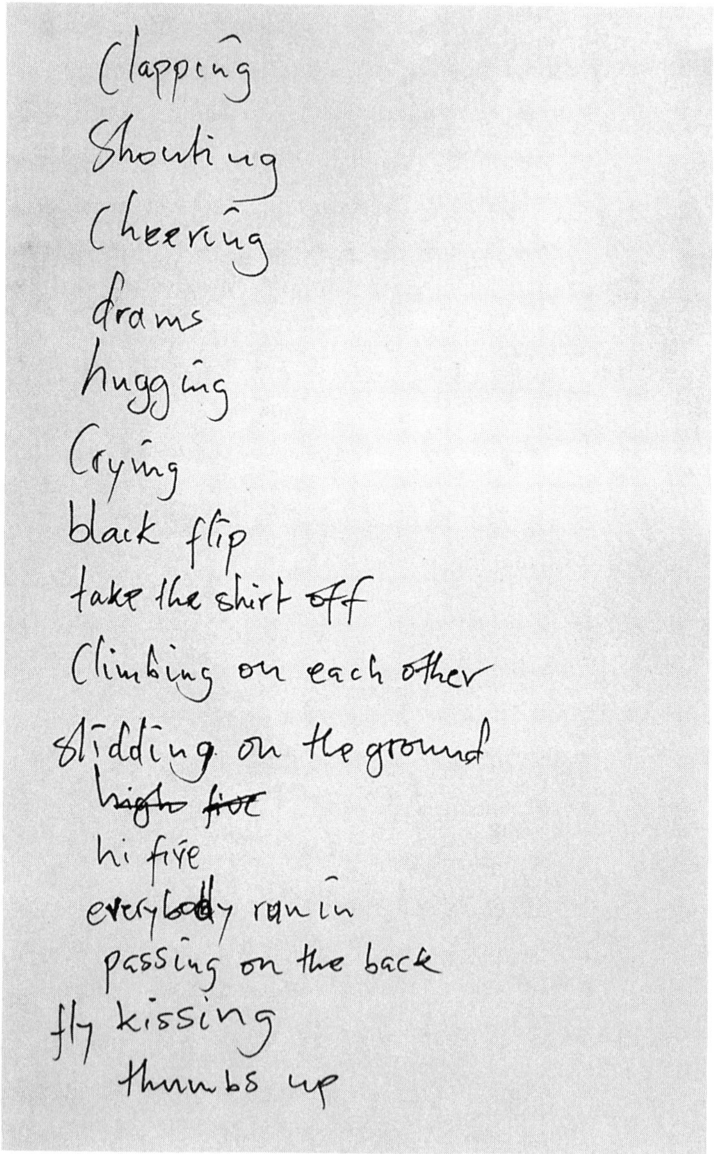

Clapping
Shouting
Cheering
drams
hugging
Crying
black flip
take the shirt off
Climbing on each other
slidding on the ground
highs five
hi five
everybody run in
passing on the back
fly kissing
thumbs up

Figure 4.5. Diverse forms of celebration.

We love the world

So we have to make it a better place

In this world

There are many people

Who need our help and our love[7]

Part Four: Looking Forward

Once we have looked back and celebrated a collective goal that has *already* been scored, it's much easier to look forward and to consider the following questions:

- What is the next goal you are planning to achieve?
- How is this team going to overcome any adversities or problems it is facing?
- What strategies and forms of team work will you use?
- What sort of training will be necessary?
- What advice will the coach give?

Again, sporting metaphors and imagery can help us, as illustrated in Figure 4.6.

Sometimes using the metaphor of a Team of Life can make it easier to think about our lives. Many profound conversations have emerged through this process. Where once there were no words, people begin to articulate what is important to them in life. For instance, in an Aboriginal community in Central Australia, one of the women of the community, Nerissa Meneri, named her softball Team of Life "When Love Comes Your Way, You Catch It."

These days, I am in a different sort of training. My sister has kids, and she's training me and my other sisters how

Figure 4.6. Looking forward to future goals.

to look after kids. I'm the youngest, and I learn by watching what she has done so that if I adopt one or two, then I will look after them in the same way that my sister is doing. When my mom and dad were drinking, my young uncle and aunty looked after us. They trained us how to show love and care for each other. In softball, you practice by throwing the ball around. It's the same in life. We practice by throwing love and care to each other. And the outfielders—my mother, cousins, brothers, and sisters—do the same. In life, when love comes your way, you catch it. If your brother or sister throws you love, you catch it and put it in your heart.

Other Metaphors

If the "club" or "team" metaphor does not easily fit you, there are many other metaphors you can use. Some people like to think of their "band" or "orchestra" of life; others consider whom they would want to take with them in walking the "journey of life" (see Chapter 5).

Getting in Touch with Better Judgment

It's also possible to engage in re-membering conversations about significant figures in our history without using a metaphor. There are times in all of our lives that we act in ways that are against our own better judgment. We all sometimes do things that we are likely to regret at a later time. In these moments, re-membering practices can assist us in getting back in touch with our better judgment. This was true for James Johnson when he met with Michael White, as illustrated in the following story.[8]

James and Elaine Johnson, along with their three children, were referred because teachers from the local primary school that the children attended had some concerns about the behavior of the two older children. Interactions that had been witnessed between the parents and the children, and particularly between Mr. Johnson and his elder son, Patrick, had reinforced these concerns. In the opinion of these teachers, what they had witnessed constituted emotional abuse, and this was something that they believed required immediate attention for the sake of the children's well-being. After a series of conversations and negotiations, an agreement was reached with the parents to have them attend an appointment with me, "just to see how it goes."

I understood from the very limited information I had been given about this situation prior to the appointment that James was relatively reluctant to take this step. This understanding was immediately reinforced at first contact. When I introduced myself in the waiting room, Elaine seemed happy to meet me, the children appeared not to notice my presence, and James gave me a decidedly cool reception. As we walked upstairs to my room, I pondered how everyone's assumptions about this meeting might be addressed in a way that would make it possible for James to be present to our conversation.

When we entered the room, James and Elaine took a seat, and the three children began to busy themselves with my collection of stuffed toys. I attempted to engage James and Elaine in a conversation about our different understandings of what the meeting was to be about, but I quickly lost James. The children were engaged in some argument over the stuffed toys, and James had begun shouting orders at them. He was particularly demeaning of Patrick and called him a lot of bad names. I then lost Elaine as well. She had joined James in shouting at the children. Two of the children were now crying. This turn of events weighed on me heavily, so I found some space in which to begin asking James and Elaine a series of questions about their experiences of parenting.

I wanted to know whether or not there had been times in this demanding task when they had found themselves somewhat stressed, maybe even at their wits' end. Before they responded to this question, I said that although in my entire career I hadn't found parents who could respond to questions of this sort in the negative, I was open to the possibility that James and Elaine would be the first to do so. They glanced in each other's direction. Elaine then responded to the question in the affirmative, and soon after James followed suit.

"At these times," I asked, "have either of you ever found yourself saying or doing anything in your relationship with your children that went against your better judgment? Or that compromised your wisdom? Or that in some way contradicted how you want things to be in your relationship with your children?"

Again, before they responded to this question, I informed Elaine and James that I hadn't yet managed to find parents who could answer this question in the negative, but that I was open to the possibility that they would be the first to do so. After a brief pause, Elaine again responded in the affirmative, and again, James followed suit.

These responses presented me with the opportunity to interview Elaine and James about this better judgment—about this parenting wisdom that they got separated from when their relationship with their children was tough and things were not going well. I encouraged them to express their ideas about this better judgment; I wanted to know what it looked like when it was effective in shaping their interaction with their children. Elaine led the way in responding to these questions, but she was supported by James in this. On an occasion or two, I managed to consult Patrick about this account of his parents' better judgment: "When things get stressed between you and your parents, would it be better if they handled this by staying true to this better judgment that they are now talking about, or would it work better for them to lose this?"

Following some clarification of this question, Patrick's response was instantaneous and unequivocal. As children *invariably do on these occasions, he voted for the better judgment. Although better judgment became more significantly described as the interview progressed, I knew that for James it remained a relatively thin trace, and that because of this, it might not be strong enough to influence his further interactions with his children.*

Toward the end of our meeting, I began to ask James and Elaine about the history of this better judgment. How had they reached their conclusions about parenting wisdom? Had their experiences of parenting and of being parented played a part in clarifying for them what constituted better judgment in their interactions with children? If so, what were these experiences? If not, what experiences had they taken their clues from? What else had contributed to the sort of realizations that had helped them to distinguish how they wanted things to be for them in their relationships with their children from how they didn't want things to be? Both Elaine and James were interested in a return visit, so we scheduled a time for this, and I wrote a list of these and similar questions for them to take away and reflect on between meetings.

Elaine and James showed up at the second meeting without the children. They had decided that they wanted an uncluttered space in which to talk about the questions that I had left them with at the end of the first meeting. Elaine opened the conversation with an account of the history of her connection to better judgment. This included some "discoveries" that she had made during the interval between meetings, and her thoughts about the implications of these in her relationship with the children. James sat quietly listening as this account unfolded. Then it was his turn. He said that he didn't have much to tell. Both parents had been abusive of him. He couldn't recall good experiences of being parented. He had learned some things from Elaine over the years, but he said it was more likely that he would "lose it" with his children than it was that Elaine would, and that he had more difficulty sticking with better judgment than she did.

Despite the fact that James was now taking a position against those practices of parenting that stood outside the realm of better judgment, I was concerned that having "nothing much to tell" would restrict him in the exploration of better-judgment options in his relationship with his children— that this alternative account of parenting might remain a thin trace, one not significantly influential of his actions as a father. In response to this concern, I said that it was my understanding that conceptions of better judgment in parenting practices don't come out of the blue, and asked if it would be okay for me to join with him in further exploration of the history of his conceptions. James said that he was open to this idea, and so began a series of exploratory conversations that took up the rest of that session and extended to the next, which James chose to attend alone.

There were two very significant outcomes of these exploratory conversations. One was an explicit recognition and acknowledgement of Elaine's contribution of options for James's expression of better judgment. The other outcome was that James recalled an episode of his personal history that he had never before spoken of and that had nearly been lost to memory. He informed me that when he had been a child he would leave home as early as possible on school day mornings because his household was not a good place for him to be at those times. On the way to school, he would walk by the home of Frank, a school friend, and then retrace his steps to wait outside the front gate until he estimated that the members of Frank's household were up and dressed and having breakfast. At that point, if he hadn't already been discovered standing there, James would go and knock on the front door. He would always be shown in by Frank's parents, Mr. and Mrs. Georgio, and invited to join the family at the breakfast table. Mr. Georgio would always give him watermelon. This was a treat.

I asked James why it was that he was telling me this story. What was it about this experience that was important to him? He said that perhaps it provided some answer to my questions about the history of this better judgment in parenting practices—perhaps this was his introduction to other possibilities in parenting. I wanted to know from James what ways of parenting had been expressed by Mrs. and Mr. Georgio at these times, and why it was that James so related to these expressions. James was at a loss for words. He had no names for these expressions. I thus asked him to tell me more stories about Mr. and Mrs. Georgio's interactions with him and with their own children. I acted as the scribe. I then went over my notes with James, and together we speculated about names for what was being expressed by these parents. "Understanding," "respect," "tolerance," "kindness," and "giving" were just some of the names that James settled on.

"It is good to get more of a sense of what you stand for, James," I remarked.

"Well, it is good for me to get a better sense of what I stand for, too," came the response.

After talking with James about his thoughts on why it was important to get more of a sense of what he stood for in regard to the practices of parenting, I wondered if it would be helpful to him to achieve an even better familiarity with this. He said he thought it would. In discussing the options for this, I said that I had an idea that might seem a little far-fetched, but wanted to suggest it anyway: "What about the idea of getting in touch with Frank and his parents so that we might have the opportunity to more directly learn about these parenting practices that struck such a chord for you?" James was initially open-mouthed at the idea but began to warm to it as we approached the end of our meeting. He departed saying that he would try to contact Frank and his parents, but that he wasn't at all sure he would be able to locate their where-abouts, as he hadn't "seen Frank for eons."

James called me three days later. He had located Frank. Mr. Georgio had died of heart failure six years before, but James did have Mrs. Georgio's telephone number. He asked me to write it down.

"Why?" I asked.

"So you can contact her."

"Why me?"

"Don't know if I feel up to this myself," replied James.

"Do you really want me to go ahead with this?" I asked.

"Yes."

"You're sure?"

"Yes."

"Okay. So what do you want me to tell her?"

"Tell her everything. The lot. Mary's her first name."

Not satisfied with this, I went over with James what I thought might be helpful for Mrs. Georgio to know. He approved this, and I made the call that afternoon. I was relieved when Mary Georgio said that not only did she remember James, but she had often found herself wondering what had become of him. She had vivid memories of his visits to her home early on those school mornings.

Mary reminisced a little, and then she told me what James had never known. Mary had figured that James was being subject to abuse at home and had talked to the school and to some neighbors about what action to take on this realization. This was more than two decades ago, well before the conspiracy of silence over abuse was broken, and the little advice Mary received from these consultations encouraged her to do nothing: 'There's not enough to go on. If you act on this, it will just make it worse for James. He won't be able to keep his friendship with Frank. And he won't be allowed to visit your home ever again." Mary and her husband, Bob, were anguished. What could they do? The only course that seemed available to them was to provide James with whatever nurturing they could in the limited opportunities that were available to them. Mary remembered the watermelon and told me that it was not by chance that Bob developed the habit of serving James with generous helpings of this and other treats.

And there was more that James didn't know. The fact that James was frequently discovered at the front gate in the early mornings was not by chance either. Mary and Bob had made it their business to be aware of his presence and would discover him by "accident" as they went to fetch the paper or turn on the garden hose. They had told James that he could come right in and knock on the door instead of waiting outside, but he never took them up on this invitation. So Bob and Mary went right on discovering him. I informed Mary of James's parenting project and of how she and Bob had figured in our discussions of this, and I asked if she would be prepared to join in our endeavor by coming to a meeting in my office. Her response was, "I would be delighted."

I immediately called James. As I recounted my conversation with Mary, he became very emotional. When I got to the parts that he hadn't known—about Mary and Bob's consciousness of what he had been going through, about their anguish, about what they had resolved to do about the situation, about the watermelon, and about his being discovered in the mornings—James started to sob. Then, not able to speak, he hung up. I was crying too. Over the next thirty-five minutes, James called back four times. He then went off to talk to Elaine about it all.

The meeting with Mary went ahead. In her presence, I had the opportunity to ask James questions about the project that he had embarked upon—to understand more about what he stood for in his parenting practices, and to stay closer to these understandings in his relationship with his children. I also asked him to review how it was that, in explorations of the history of this better judgment, a line was traced back to the contribution of Mary and Bob Georgio. Mary was visibly touched by what James had to say. When James stopped speaking, I asked Mary if she would speak of her experience of this telling. She said it was "wonderful for her to hear," and that she felt so relieved to know that what she and Bob had done in response to James's plight "had been for something." She wished that Bob could have joined us in this meeting, as she felt it would have meant a lot to him, too.

Mary also said that although she understood that every-thing hadn't turned out how James might have hoped it would in his relationship with his children, nonetheless it was an extraordinary thing that James had taken up, into his life, *some of these other understandings about what it meant to parent children, despite all that he had gone through as a child. It was clear that James was warmed by this. I asked Mary if we could ask her some questions about what it was that she and Bob had stood for in their parenting, about the know-how that the two of them had expressed as parents, and about the history of that knowledge in their own lives. In response to the last question, Mary spoke of various figures in their personal histories and powerfully invoked the image of her maternal grandmother, Maria, who had been a strong voice on matters of fairness and respect.*

I encouraged James to formulate a number of better-judgment proposals for how he might respond to his children when things were going off track, and James, Mary, and I then met with Elaine and the children to catch them up on these developments and consult them about these proposals for action. The feedback that James received was very reinforcing and provided clarity around which of the proposals would be most likely to have a desirable outcome for Elaine and the children. I wondered aloud how James might stay in touch with these proposals under stressful circumstances. Various suggestions were offered. Mary said that it would be fine for James to call her at these times. This was the option that James took up.

At follow-up I learned that things had been working out much better all around in the Johnson family. It wasn't that there hadn't been some difficult moments, but James and Elaine had stood together through them, not allowing themselves to become separated from respectful parenting practices. James had spent some time informing the children's teachers of developments in his project, and they had been supportive of him in this. These teachers also reported that the children appeared less stressed and were becoming more confident in classroom and schoolyard contexts. The Johnson family had become part of the Georgio family's extended kin network, and James and Frank's reclaimed friendship was looking more and more like a brotherhood.

Reconnecting with Your Own Better Judgment

In all of our lives, there are times when we lose touch with our own "better judgment."

- When are some of the times, or what are some of the contexts, in which you lose touch with your "better judgment"? (This doesn't have to be in relation to parenting; it could be in relation to friendship, work, or any aspect of your life.)
- What is the history of your better judgment? Who introduced you to better judgment in the first place? How did they do this? What might they suggest in terms of ways of staying in touch with better judgment now?
- In thinking about the history of better judgment and who introduced you to it, what proposals for action could you put in place in your life now?
- If you were to take these steps, what would it mean for you and others in your life? And what would it mean for those who introduced you to better judgment? If they were present, what might they say to you about this? What do you think it would mean to them that you are doing what you can to carry on this tradition of better judgment?

Indeed, what do you think it might mean to James that his story and the story of the Johnson and Georgio families might strengthen better judgment in the lives of others?

Looking Back, Looking Forward

So far in this book we have considered how the stories of our lives influence who we are and who we can become. We've discussed problem stories of identity ("lonely boy," "good for nothing") and preferred stories ("a songwriter on top of the world," "the kindest person I know"). We've considered how the person is not the problem; the problem is the problem. We've explored how we can find the right audiences for our stories. In this chapter, we've thought about our life as a team or club and explored who we would choose as our teammates. And we've tried to get in touch with our better judgment and to recall who introduced us to it. Now it's time to make preparations for a journey, because rewriting the stories of our lives is like undertaking an expedition.

Notes

1. The story of Louise is taken from the book *Narratives of Therapists' Lives* by Michael White (1997). It has been edited slightly from the original and is republished with permission.
2. The Team of Life was developed on a trip to Uganda. The members of the Dulwich Centre Team were Cheryl White, Michael White, Eileen Hurley, and David Denborough. We had been invited to Uganda by REPSSI (see www.repssi.org). For more information about the Team of Life, see Denborough, 2008, 2012b, or www.dulwichcentre.com.au/team-of-life.html
3. The Arabic team sheet was developed through the work of Nihaya Abu-Rayyan.
4. Dwayne's Team of Life was facilitated by Eileen Hurley. It is included here with permission. Dwayne is a pseudonym.
5. Julie-Anne's Team of Life was facilitated by Eileen Hurley. It is included here with permission. Julie-Anne is a pseudonym.

6. The team sheets created by Tony and other young refugees to Australia were made at a gathering in Adelaide that was organized by Families SA Refugee Services. Nagita Kaggwa was particularly influential. The team sheets are offered here with permission.

7. Copyright © 2010 by Tony Kamara.

8. The story of James is taken from the book *Narratives of Therapists' Lives* by Michael White (1997). It has been edited slightly from the original and is republished with permission.

CHAPTER 5

Life as a Journey: Migrations of Identity

LIFE CAN BE likened to a journey. Often it involves plotting courses to destinations that we might not have predicted and navigating transitions that might not always be comfortable. Invariably life's journeys lead us to become different than we were when we first set off.

The Power to Our Journeys group, mentioned in Chapter 3, consisted of people who were reclaiming their lives from hostile voices (sometimes referred to as the auditory hallucinations of schizophrenia). The group's logo was Mount Kilimanjaro.

Quite some years ago, Sue, one of the members of our group, climbed to the top of this mountain. In one of our meetings she remarked that getting her life back from the hostile voices was a journey that was not dissimilar to the climb to the top of Mount Kilimanjaro. "It is hard work," she said, "but with the right preparations and provisions, a good map of the terrain, access to forecasts that make it possible to predict the weather ahead, and the appropriate support systems, it can be done." We all embrace this philosophy. We will continue to equip ourselves with these tools and to develop the sort of support systems that will make it possible for us to see this journey through. (Brigitte, Sue, Mem, and Veronika, 1997, p. 209)

Once we begin the process of rewriting the stories of our lives, there are always ups and downs. Problems that have been around for a while don't just up and leave. It can be really important to prepare for the journey.

Consider for a moment the experiences of women who leave and then stay out of relationships in which men are abusing them. This process can be a particularly difficult journey:

There are many important considerations that make it difficult for women to leave these relationships . . . there are considerations of an economic nature, and those that relate to the existence of few options for alternative housing, lack of support from relatives and friends, threats and harassment from the men concerned, and so on. But there is another important consideration . . . Usually, at the point of separation, and/or in the period leading up to this point, women who are being abused by their men partners experience rising expectations— expectations that, through this course of action, that is, separation, they might emerge from the terror and the despair that has become so much part of their daily existence, and expectations that they might find themselves arriving at a degree of wellbeing. However, despite the rising expectations that are experienced up to the point of separation and for a short time after this, wherever these women find themselves following separation—whether this be in their own accommodation, in refuges or staying with friends or relatives—there is a very real risk early in this journey that they will turn back to an unchanged violent situation. And, a great percentage of women in fact do this.

So often, shortly after leaving the man who is violent, women begin to lose their sense of relief at having escaped, as well as their hopefulness about new options and possibilities for their own lives and for the lives of their children, and find themselves sinking back into despair. Very soon they find themselves in a "trough," one characterised by confusion, disorientation, profound insecurity, and a sense of personal failure. Women's experience of this trough can be so overwhelming that they can find themselves feeling even worse than they did prior to leaving the abusive man. This development is often read as "I am worse off than before," and for many women this plays a significant role in forming a decision to turn back to an unchanged violent situation, despite the alarm and the protest that this decision arouses in concerned others. (*White, 1995a, p. 98*)

There are, however, other ways to understand this "trough-like" experience that make it more possible to proceed. Working to leave and to stay out of a relationship in which you have been subjected to violence can be seen as a "migration of identity":

When women take steps to break free from abuse, they are doing a great deal more than breaking from the ongoing trauma, they are doing a great deal more than breaking from a familiar social network, and they are doing a great deal more than stepping into material insecurity—although all of this alone is more than enough to have to deal with at any time in one's life. At this time, women are also embarking on a migration of identity . . . And in any migration, there is a "betwixt and between" space where confusion and disorientation reigns, and often nothing seems manageable any more, not even one's relationship with one's children. It is in this space that women are vulnerable to a sense of total incompetence and personal failure, to feelings of desperation and acute despair. (*White, 1995a, pp. 99–100*)

If we are undertaking any significant journey, it can be vital to have a map to show us how to navigate the terrain and to forecast some of the ups and downs we are likely to face. To undertake a migration of identity, therefore, it can be significant to map out the journey:

> If women have the opportunity to map their experience of the descent into this trough of confusion and disorientation as part of a process, if they have the opportunity to map this as a part of an ongoing journey, rather than interpret it as regress, then they are less at risk of turning back to an unchanged violent context. If women can understand these experiences as the products of a migration of identity, it becomes more possible for them to persevere with their journey despite the disorientation and the confusion. Such acts of mapping assist women to place their distress within the context of progress, to stand by and to hold onto the idea that the future might hold something different for them, to hold onto their hopes, to their expectations for a better life, to keep in sight the horizon of another world. (*White, 1995a, p.100*)

Figure 5.1 shows a graph created by a woman named Betty to represent her migration of identity.[1]

When we look at Betty's graph, we see a migration of identity that took eleven months. These processes take time; in fact, Michael White used to inform women that the minimum time required for these migrations of identity is about nine months. We can also see in Betty's graph that her feelings of confusion, disorganization, and disorientation in the first few months after separation were not a sign of going backward

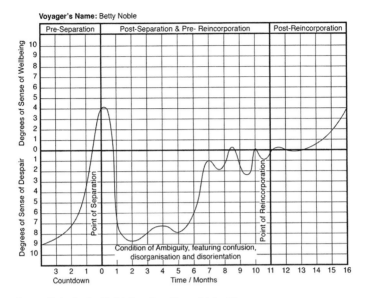

Figure 5.1. Betty Noble's migration of identity.

but actually an indication of progress. Creating a migration-of-identity map or graph like this can help us to be less vulnerable to acute despair. If we are feeling confused, it can help us see that this is part of a longer migration; in fact, we can even predict that there will be times of profound disorientation and understand that this is part of the journey.

Creating drawings of these migrations also makes it easier for women to share their experiences with one another and to compare where they are in their migration: "Look, this is where Betty was at the three-month mark. I am three months into this. Where do I think I am on this graph? Where would I locate my present position?" The answer might be, "Well, I think I'm feeling worse than Betty did at this point," or "I don't think I'm feeling quite as desperate as Betty did at this point." Either way, these comparisons can assist people in plotting their own progress and making their own migration graphs.

Women who are undergoing a migration of identity away from a relationship of abuse might also interview others who have been through migrations:

> These might be migrations similar to their own, or other kinds of migrations, including geographical migrations. In Australia, there would be very few people who would not know anyone who has migrated, and most would know someone who found the migration process difficult—who found the going hard to the extent that they nearly turned back, or perhaps wished they could have turned back. In interviewing others about migration experiences, women can identify what sustained them through this, and they can develop knowledges about what circumstances are most favourable to perseverance. Further, they can get a keener sense of how far down the track they might be before feeling that they are breaking from some of the insecurity, confusion and disorientation that is associated with these migrations. Planning a celebration at the point of arrival at the journey's end can also assist in establishing these circumstances. This planning can extend all the way through to putting together the invitation list, and even to preparing the invitations. (*White, 1995a, pp. 103–104*)

Your Own Migration-of-Identity Map

Are you also involved in a migration of identity? Are you trying to leave certain ways of living behind and embrace a new lifestyle? If so, perhaps you would like to map this on the grid provided in Figure 5.2. Look again at Betty Noble's map and then create your own. Make sure you include some of the ups and downs that you have already experienced, and then, perhaps in pencil, you can also map out the sorts of ups and downs that might occur in the future. As you pass through the next nine months or so, you can keep revising your map.

If you know someone who has been through a process of migration from another country, perhaps you can ask them to map out the process they went through. You can then compare and contrast your "journeys."

Figure 5.3 shows another example of a migration-of-identity map.[2] This is from a Palestinian woman, Amal, who has recently been released from prison. Her narrative therapist, Nihaya Abu-Rayyan, uses the metaphors of the different seasons (autumn, winter, spring, summer) to represent the different

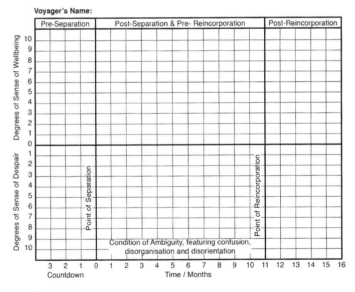

Figure 5.2. Create your own migration-of-identity map.

stages of the prison experience. Sometimes passing through major changes in life is like passing through all the seasons.

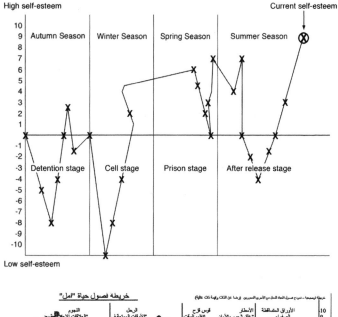

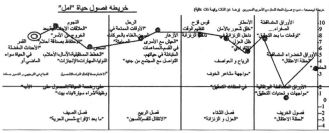

Figure 5.3. Amal's migration through the Seasons of Life.

Predicting the Backlash

In undertaking journeys, it can be particularly important to predict those moments when we might feel as if we are plunging backward or have slipped back to the very beginning.

Unless we predict these moments, they can make us feel as if we are a failure.

Maria, an adult survivor of childhood sexual abuse, describes the significance of predicting these times:

> As you go along through migrations of identity, a lot of things become clear. One of these involves backlash and how important it is to predict when hard times might come and how you might be able to deal with them. Being aware of the tricks of abuse has made an enormous difference to me. I once thought that the "voice of abuse" spoke the truth. It was like a commentary running in my head. When I named it "the voice of abuse," this made all the difference. I could then separate myself from it. I could come up with my own understandings about what is true for me. This has been a revelation. It is about reversing the control. The events of the past no longer control me; in fact, in many ways, I have increasing control over them.[3]

Notice how Maria has externalized the "voice of abuse" and how this is assisting her in discerning its tricks and determining when it is most likely to lash back at her. This concept of backlash can be very helpful. No doubt, as you begin to reclaim your life from the effects of whatever problems you are enduring, there will be times of backlash—times when the problem makes a comeback. Predicting these moments and working out plans in advance can make all the difference.

The members of the Power to Our Journeys group were experts at this. They knew that in order to undertake the profound journey of reclaiming their lives from the effects of the hostile voices and visions of schizophrenia, they would need to be ready for times of backlash. With the assistance of Michael White, they created the following document.[4]

Naming the Backlash for What It Is

by Sue, Mem, Veronika, and Brigitte

In many ways the voices are quite predictable in their actions. Whenever we take a new step in life, or subject ourselves to pressures, or whenever we are having a really great time, like playing a beautiful piece of music and feeling proud of ourselves, the voices get unsettled. In fact, engaging in anything that makes us a little bigger in the world disturbs them profoundly. We upset their applecart, and they then endeavor to exercise power over our lives to turn us back.

Whenever the voices get into a slinging match, and get on our cases, they are engaging in what best could be described as backlash. They engage in this backlash in their attempts to silence us, to make us less visible in the world, and to recruit us into hurting our own lives and into destroying our connections with others. In these efforts, the voices have to talk rubbish, but they can be very convincing nonetheless.

It is very important for us to recognize a backlash for what it is. These experiences of a backlash are not experiences of failure. They speak more to how our successes shake the voices up. Backlashes are proof of our success in the steps that we are taking in life. And naming the backlash for what it is, is to steal its thunder.

We are now all developing an increasing ability to predict these backlashes, and these predictions turn out to be particularly important. If we can predict a backlash ahead of its arrival, we can prepare ourselves for it. We can organize support from friends, plan nurturing rituals, stock pleasurable things to eat and drink, and do other things that have to do with pampering ourselves some. We can also get ready by going over with others the various tactics that we predict the voices may engage in to punish us.

In fact, the prediction of the backlash is quite vital, because if we are not prepared, then the backlash is more likely to have the effect that the voices desire. And this is not good. How would you like to be subject to five blaring radios, ten television sets tuned simultaneously to four TV stations, two video recorders running continuously, and half a dozen symphony orchestras powering away, and not be able to tune any of these in quite well?

Although these steps that we take in life do make us vulnerable to these backlashes, we do know that they challenge and eventually shrink the voices' power, even if we don't realize this at the time. We know that "from little things big things come."

We've been very creative in the work that we have done together and separately to diminish the power of these backlashes. For example, one of our group has tried understanding and developing an appreciation of the fact that these voices are like people who have hassles and take it out on others. Another member of our group used realizations that the voices really couldn't get her because they have no arms and legs. Yet another group member decided to go on the initiative and went out looking for them and even cooked meals for them. But they never showed up. We all have engaged in humor as an antidote, and this has at times been very effective.

We hereby declare that we have the knowledges that are necessary in handling backlashes, and we will remain committed to predicting these and naming them for what they are in our ongoing work to reclaim our lives.

Planning for the Backlash

In the following space, it may be useful to note the times when backlash is most likely to visit your life:

_____

_____

_____

_____

Having done so, now you might like to note the preparations you could make in advance of these times of backlash so that the backlash is less effective at encouraging you to abandon hope and turn back.

_____

_____

_____

_____

Mapping the Journey of Life

Some people have found it helpful to create a broader map of the "Journey of Life"[5] (see Figure 5.4). This involves taking a large sheet of paper and drawing a winding pathway. At the midpoint of the path, draw a circle. To the left of this circle, the pathway is the "road already traveled." To the right is "the path yet to come." Write these phrases in the appropriate places, or alternatively you can use the following template.

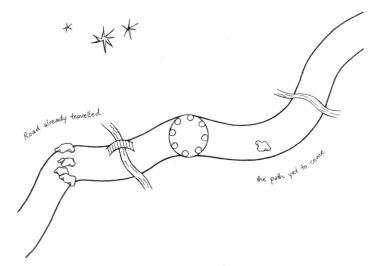

Figure 5.4. Mapping the Journey of Life.

Part One: Looking Back

1. Where You Have Come From

At the starting point of the path, note where you have come from. Include such things as places, ancestors, culture, language, and/or spirituality. These are like the roots of your Tree of Life (Chapter I). Consider the following questions and record the answers in some way at the beginning of your path:

- Who traveled first to make it possible for you to start this journey?
- What are the gifts that they gave you that you are carrying with you on this journey?

2. Your circle of support

Who are your companions on this journey (alive or in your heart)? These might be individuals, or they might be groups, communities, or organizations. Include people of different generations. You can also include spiritual figures, invisible friends, pets, and so on. Your circle will include the people from your team or club of life (Chapter 4). In the circle that you drew initially at the midpoint of the path, write the names of everyone you have chosen. If you like, you may paste in photos or draw pictures of them. This is your "circle of support."

3. Values, Beliefs, and Principles

Around the circle of support, write down some of the key values, beliefs, and principles that guide you on the journey of life. These values are like our compass. They guide us on our journey. Where or whom have they come from?

4. Favorite Places

Along the road that you have already traveled, draw or list some of the favorite places you have been on this journey so far.

5. Milestones

Along the road already traveled, what are some of the key things you have already accomplished on this journey? Draw two of these. How were these things accomplished? Who played a part?

6. Obstacles Overcome and Rivers Crossed

Along the road already traveled, draw rocks (or a mountain) and a river to symbolize two obstacles that you (or you and your circle of support) have *already* overcome on your journey of life. Indicate how you overcame, avoided, or got around the obstacles and how you crossed the river. How did you do this? Who helped?

7. Survival Kit

Toward the top of the page, draw your survival kit. Within it, write down what helped you during the difficult times. What things have you turned to for strength? These could be values, skills, people, customs, beliefs, proverbs, songs, and so forth. You might like to include here the survival skills you wrote about in Chapter 2.

Part Two: Looking Forward

Now it is time to look toward the future—the "path yet to come."

8. Where You Are Heading

Toward the end of the path yet to come, write down some of your hopes, dreams, and wishes. These might be for yourself, your friends, your community, or the next generation. You may wish to refer to the branches on your Tree of Life (Chapter I). How long have you had these hopes, dreams, or wishes? How have you held on to them? Who has helped?

9. Places You Wish to See

Along the path yet to come, name some places you (or other people in your circle of support) wish to see on the rest of your journey of life. These might also be places you wish to show others.

10. Things You Wish to Make Happen

Look back at some of the milestones you have already achieved and then, along the path yet to come, mark three

future milestones you and your circle of support are aiming
for. These should be achievable steps–things you wish to
make happen. Include one in relation to your own life, one for
your community, and one for the next generation.

11. Gifts You Wish to Give Others

Look back to some of the gifts you identified as having
been given to you and then mark on your future path some
gifts you wish to give or share with others. Alternatively, perhaps there are things that you were not given in your life that
you would like to pass on to others. Include gifts you wish to
give adults and gifts you wish to give to children.

12. Obstacles to Overcome and Rivers to Cross

Along the path yet to come, draw a rock or mountain to
symbolize one obstacle that you (or others you care about)
may face in the future and one river that you may have to
cross. How will you be able to tell when these challenges
are coming up? How will you and your circle of support try
to avoid, get around, or overcome these difficulties? Write
your response next to the obstacles and river on the path
yet to come.

How will you stay strong as you face these troubles? Look
back at your survival kit. Will you use similar tools or something different? If you will use different tools, add these to
your survival kit.

13. Traveling Songs

What songs will your circle of support be singing or playing
as you travel forward? Mark along the side of your path the

songs you will be taking with you. Why these particular songs? What do they mean to you? If you have a recording of any of these songs, play them as you proceed with Part Three of the Journey of Life exercise.

Part Three: Looking Down at Your Journey (Like an Eagle)

14. Good Memories

As you move along the path yet to come, what are some good memories that you will take with you into the future? Draw these as stars along your journey.

Describe these good memories. Include the sounds, sights, tastes, touches, or smells they are associated with. Who played a part in these memories? How and when do you remember these times?

Why is each of these memories important to you? What does it offer to you and your circle of support? What will it continue to offer in the future? Place your responses to these questions inside or alongside the stars.

15. Naming Your Journey

Give your path a name to symbolize what this Journey of Life means to you.

16. A Message to Others

Look back over everything that you have spoken about. If you were to share a message, a proverb, a story, or a song to a younger person just starting out on their journey, what would it be? What is one lesson you have learned that you would like to pass on to others?

Louise's Journey

Figure 5.5 represents the Journey of Louise, whose story of holding a re-membering ritual was told in Chapter 4. The name of Louise's journey is "Making a safer world for children"[6]

Circle of support: My friend Pat, my Aunt Helen, my counselor Jane, and Pauline, the psychiatric nurse who has stood with me through the worst times. The two colored-in circles represent me and my mother.

The values that guide me: Friendship, protection, doing no harm, and never giving up. These are the four directions of my compass. They guide me on my way. Aunt Helen and Pat help me to hold this compass sometimes.

Survival kit/basket: When I was climbing through mountains of cruelty, it was the confidence of others (especially Pat and Pauline) in me that kept me going. And when I was struggling to cross a river of loneliness, it was the beauty of music and nature that kept me company.

Where I am heading: To a place where all children are safe . . . might take us a while to get there!

Places I wish to see: New York City!

Obstacles to overcome, rivers to cross: When I start doing social work with families in which abuse is taking place, I know it will be tough. But it's what I want to do.

Travelling songs: The "Four Last Songs" by Richard Strauss bring me a sense of peace whenever I play them.

A message to young women: If I were to send a message to another young woman before she took the first steps on her journey, I would say: "Dear sister, it is normal when you are on a journey to face difficulties. There's always good luck and bad

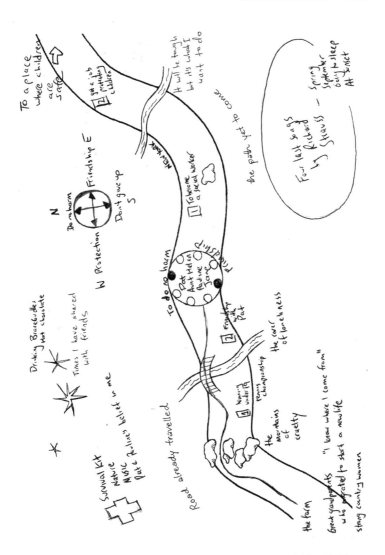

Figure 5.5. Louise's Journey of Life: Making a Safer World for Children.

*luck along the way. Whatever difficulty you are facing, please
don't blame yourself. Just try your best and talk with others
along the way. Don't give up . . . I am waiting for you just a
little bit further along the path."*

*Good memories: These are times when I have been able to
help others and times I have shared with friends. I'm thinking
especially of the trip that Pat and I took together when I just had
to get away. These are stars that light my journey.*

Creating Your Journey of Life

If you create your Journey of Life, you may simply want to
keep it as a reference point for yourself. As you work through
other chapters in this book, you may choose to add to it.
Alternatively, you may choose to create your Journey of Life
with a friend. If so, you can ask each other the questions
along the way. At the end, you can have an unveiling ritual
to honor all that you have seen so far along the journey of
your life as well as your hopes for the path yet to come.

The Words of Voyagers

It seems appropriate to end this chapter with the words of
people who know a lot about undertaking migrations of identity. The following account is from Jussey Verco regarding the
work of the group Silent Too Long, whose members are all
survivors of childhood sexual abuse.[7]

*The process of moving from negative ideas about identity to
more positive ones can be a long process and can have ups and
downs. Breaking away from negative ideas about your identity
and creating a new, more positive sense of yourself involves
moving from the known into the unknown. Once women have*

become freed up from self-blame and self-hatred and before they have become re-grounded in a positive sense of identity, they go through a betwixt-and-between stage which has both wonderful and terrifying aspects. Everything that they once thought they knew becomes questioned. Many women have told us that as they step into new understandings of who they are, they learn to say no to various things that once they would have always agreed to do. This has meant that along the way, some women have lost contact with friends and even family.

In our experience, mapping out this migration of identity can be of great assistance. We find it important to predict that women will have times when the "voice of abuse" will lash back at them, as well as times when they will feel stronger and more connected to good ideas about themselves. By predicting the hard times, the women realize when difficulties do arise that they are not going crazy and that they have not gone back to square one and instead can recall the ideas and strategies they have identified for just such occasions. This can connect women with their own abilities to care for themselves.

As women move through this process of healing, they make predictions and forecasts and plot their journey along the way. At the end of each session, we give women a map and get them to take it home and to plot where they think they are in terms of their migration of identity. These maps are then constantly available to be consulted, reviewed, and amended.

Migrations of identity in relation to the effects of sexual abuse can be long journeys. And yet, over the years, women have demonstrated time and again how these migrations can be made. Having others around to assist in the process, making preparations for difficult times, and having justifiable outrage as a respected companion all make the process of

*reclaiming one's life from the effects of sexual abuse consid-
erably more manageable.*

*In the process, many survivors also make significant contri-
butions to supporting other women and creating greater
awareness about the issue of childhood sexual abuse. Routinely, these journeys of healing are accompanied by deliberate, creative, and courageous acts aimed toward ensuring
greater safety for all our children. These acts are often the
result of women's anger, women's outrage. What better use of
outrage could there possibly be?*

Looking Back, Looking Forward

We have now come to the midway point of this book. By
now, I hope you have a number of new ways of thinking
about your life:

- Ways of thinking about storylines of identity
- Ways of naming problems that are separate from you
- Ways of seeking out audiences for your preferred stories
- Ways of making documents and writing letters and certifi-
cates
- Ways of creating re-grading rituals
- Ways of thinking about your life as a club or team
- Ways of thinking about your life as a journey

Now might be a good time to look back on the territory we
have already covered and the writings about your life that
you have generated in response to these first chapters. Perhaps when you look back at what you wrote earlier, you will
have new realizations. Perhaps the process of rewriting and
retelling the stories of your life has already begun.

When you are ready, let's proceed.

Notes

1. The descriptions of Michael White's work with women survivors of domestic violence and Betty Noble's migration of identity map were first published in White, 1995a.

2. The maps from Nihaya Abu-Rayyan are taken from Abu-Rayyan, 2009, p. 38.

3. The quotation from Maria in relation to migrations of identity is from Silent Too Long, 2000.

4. The work of Power to Our Journeys, including the document *Naming the Backlash for What It Is*, was first published in Brigitte, Sue, Mem, and Veronika, 1997.

5. Journey metaphors have been used within narrative therapy for many years (see White, 2002a). I first shared this version of the Journey of Life with workers from REPSSI (www.repssi.org) who use a different version of this metaphor to talk with communities in Southern and Eastern Africa about child protection.

6. This journey drawing was reconstructed from Louise's story. Louise is a composite character.

7. The extract from Jussey Verco is from Verco, 2002.

Part Two

CHAPTER 6

Questioning Normality and Escaping from Failure

HAVE YOU EVER felt like a failure? As if you don't measure up as a "normal" person according to the guidelines of our time and culture? If so, you are in good company:

> The phenomenon of personal failure has grown exponentially over recent decades. Never before has the sense of being a failure to be an adequate person been so freely available to people, and never before has it been so willingly and routinely dispensed. (White, 2002b, p. 33)

This chapter is about escaping from failure. In order to revise the storylines of our lives, we may need to question "normality" and find escape routes from experiences of failure. The following pages include the perspectives of people who have experienced mental health struggles, as their stories can provide us all with special knowledge about ways to live outside the confines of what is considered normal. Their words and deeds provide options for ways of celebrating "escaping failure," questioning normality, and honoring diverse ways of living.

Denise is a twenty-four-year-old woman who made an escape from failure. I want to share a transcript of a conversation that Denise and her parents shared with Michael White.[1] I will then offer some reflections on what a difference it can make in our lives if we begin to challenge what is considered normal in our culture; if we escape from judging ourselves and others in relation to normality; if we start to honor the diversity of our lives and the lives of others; and if we start to appreciate what special knowledge we may have gained in our lives from experiences of difference or even hardship.

For now, though, let's meet Denise and her parents.

I introduced myself to Denise and her parents, Katherine and Gordon, in the waiting room. All three were apprehensive, and it was clear to me that Denise and Katherine had been crying. Denise's movements were slow and our journey to the interviewing room seemed a long one. When we were seated, Gordon and Katherine informed me of Denise's lack of enthusiasm about this appointment with me and began to speak of their concern for her. In response to this, I consulted Denise about her understanding of this appointment and the circumstances of her attendance. With an economy of words, she flatly informed me that although she'd had no wish to attend this appointment, she had not felt compelled to do so, and had decided to do this for her parents' sake.

I asked Denise if it would be okay for her parents to fill me in on their concerns for her, or whether she would prefer to speak to her understanding of these concerns. In response, and again with great economy of words, Denise said that it would work best for her if Gordon and Katherine were to speak.

In the next ten minutes I learned that Denise had been diagnosed with schizophrenia some years ago after a series of psychotic episodes, had been trialed on several different major tranquilizers, and had been hospitalized on half a dozen occasions. Although Denise was now on a medication that had relieved her of some of the more troubling aspects of her psychotic experience, her general quality of life was poor—she was quite isolated and withdrawn, often despairing, at times quite desperate, and felt generally hopeless about her future. I asked Denise if she thought that her parents had given an accurate account of how things were for her, and she nodded in affirmation.

Katherine and Gordon had made the appointment to meet with me on Denise's behalf after a recent suicide attempt. To their knowledge, this was her fifth attempt and the most life threatening of them all. Following Denise's recovery from this, she had confided to them that she felt herself to be failure as a person in every way imaginable, and that she believed that she would never get her life together.

Gordon: So that's why we made this appointment, Michael. There just has to be something else that we can do.

Katherine: Yes, Denise doesn't have a very good time of life. Do you, honey? [turning to Denise, who is now in tears] I know she feels such a failure, but she's not. And we love her so much.

Denise: [crying softly]

Katherine: I know that you didn't want to come here, and that you did it for us. [turning to Michael] Getting her out of her bedroom is very difficult on any occasion.

Michael: [turning to Denise] Your parents have now filled me in on what they are concerned about. I have done my best to check these concerns with you, and understand from your response that these concerns are mostly accurate. Would it be okay for me to ask you a few questions?

Denise: [nods]

Michael: Can you confirm what your parents are saying about feeling that you are a failure?

Denise: [shrugs, then nods in affirmation]

Michael: Can you talk about this?

Denise: [still crying softly] Don't think I can.

Michael: Would it be okay by you for me to ask your mom and dad about what they think this is like for you?

Denise: It's okay.

Michael: [to Katherine and Gordon] Would you say more about your understanding of what this is like for Denise?

Gordon: Time and again we have seen Denise set out to make something of her life, and time and again she has crashed, and everything has come undone. So, I think that this has convinced her that she is a failure as a person.

Katherine: We feel so much for her when we see these expectations crushed. We try to reassure her and tell her that it is okay, that there will be other days, but this doesn't work anymore. Now there isn't anything that we can do at these times to make her feel better. [Katherine and Denise's eyes meet, and they are both in tears.]

Michael: You mentioned expectations. What are these expectations that Denise feels that she is failing?

Katherine: Just the usual. That she will get herself together, have a life.

Michael: Expectations for what sort of life?

Katherine: You know all of those things like being independent, achieving her goals. Being able to handle herself in social situations, like having it together socially. Having a relationship, and maybe a career. All of these things.

Gordon: Yeah. Achieving her best potential.

Michael: Where do these expectations come from?

Katherine: I'm glad that you asked this question. Because it's not just from us, is it Gordon?

Gordon: We hear these expectations all of the time. People are always giving us opinions about what would be good for Denise. About what she could be doing, about what we could be doing. About what they would be doing if they were us and Denise was their daughter, and about what Denise would be doing if she was their daughter. It goes on and on. Mostly it is all pretty subtle, mostly inferences. It is everywhere, and I know that Denise has had her fair share of it.

Katherine: It is everywhere. We've tried not to join in, but we've done it too. I mean, we have also put these expectations onto Denise. *[turning to Denise]* Haven't we?

Denise: *[clearly engaged by what she is hearing, nods in affirmation]*

Katherine: We know it's not helpful. But it is so hard not to do this when we want so much for you.

Michael: What's this like for you and Gordon? How do all of these expectations affect how you feel about yourselves as parents? Do these expectations affect your own opinions of who you are as Denise's parents?

Katherine: I know that I don't feel too good about it. Gordon feels this too. We don't like to admit it, and we keep trying, but I think that we both feel like failures as parents. I hope it is okay to say this [turning to Denise], and that it isn't upsetting to you. But Denise doesn't have this sense of being a failure alone. We all have it, but just try to pretend that it isn't there.

Michael: Gordon?

Gordon: [sighs] Yeah, it's true. We don't know where to turn with this. For sure, we can't speak to other parents about it. They all seem to be doing so fine. [sighs again]

Michael: You might not be surprised to hear that I meet with a lot of people who have failed a lot of expectations and prospects for their lives. In fact, there is so much that can be failed that, some time ago, this got me interested in collecting an account of the possible failures. It would be helpful to me in my conversations with you if we could compile a list of the expectations and prospects that you sense you have failed. Who knows, there might be some new ones!

Gordon: [smiles] I could be part of that.

Katherine: [also smiling] Me, too.

Michael: Denise?

Denise: Yeah. I could help out with that.

Michael: Great! Let's get started.

Over the next thirty minutes, Denise, Katherine, and Gordon assisted me in compiling a list of the expectations and the prospects for their lives and relationships that they had a sense of failing to achieve. We also worked together to identify some of the sources that were sponsoring these expectations and prospects, and discovered these in a range of routinely offered

*opinions, judgments, conclusions, attitudes, viewpoints, infer-
ences, evaluations, and taken-for-granted assumptions about
what life is all about. Gordon, Katherine, and Denise concluded that virtually all of these were unsolicited.*

*I then took the opportunity to interview the family about
the effects of these expectations on their lives and on their
relationships, and about how these had shaped their conclusions about their identities. As this conversation evolved,
Denise began to participate more fully. These expectations
had her constantly assessing whether her thoughts and actions
were real enough, mistrusting most of what she thought and
did, questioning everything about her life, and worrying
about whether she was coming across as a "together" person.
The expectations had Katherine permanently on duty trying
to make things better for everyone, judging herself negatively
as a mother and a woman, always appraising and weighing
her words and deeds, and engaging in a reckoning of her
performance at the end of each day. The expectations had
required of Gordon that he be vigilant in his assessment of the
adequacy of his words and deeds and had significantly isolated him from friends and workmates.*

*At the second meeting, we compared the list of failed expec-
tations with a master list[2] I had been compiling over some
years. We discovered that most of the failed expectations on
their list were already present in the master list. We also discovered that there were many other expectations that Katherine, Gordon, and Denise could have subjected themselves to,
but hadn't. I wondered aloud about why it was that they hadn't
made their lives available to more of these expectations,
and why it was that they were not giving themselves the hard*

time that they could be giving themselves. Gordon, Denise and Katherine found my questions amusing and informed me that they simply hadn't thought of some of these expectations (and that if they had, they wouldn't have had a life at all), and that the others they considered just plain ridiculous.

This review had a dramatic effect on our conversation. Denise, suddenly quite animated, offered that not only had she not made herself available to many of the expectations of the master list, but that she had also "dropped" some that she had been available to. These were expectations about being a more productive person. She had decided that there was no way that she could measure up to these, and she no longer experienced such discomfort over this. "After all," Denise said, "I am entitled to a little relaxation and fun."

Michael: How did you step back from these expectations?
Denise: Just did.
Michael: It seems to be a pretty big "just did." Could you say a little more about what went into this "just did"?
Denise: Well . . . er . . . it was using my mind.
Michael: What makes it possible for you to use your mind in this way?
Denise: Well, it's like this. I have realized that sometimes I am able to use my mind to say no to these expectations. It's like I've got . . . now, what is it I've got? Let's see. Um . . .
Katherine: Is it like willpower? Like having a strong will?
Denise: Yeah. That's it. That's right. That's the word I am looking for. It's willpower.
Michael: Is willpower something about your life that is important to you?
Denise: Yeah. I guess it is. But I lose it.

Katherine: I think that she always prided herself in it.

Michael: [to Denise] What is it that guides how you use this willpower?

Denise: I don't know. I don't know. Um. It's something, for sure. What do you think, Mom?

Katherine: I think that in lots of ways you are a very accepting person. And you also value understanding. This has shown up many times before. It is like you have these principles that you won't budge on. Way back as far as I can remember, there have been so many times when you wouldn't be reacting to some of the things that you heard like lots of other people would, like everybody would expect, but you would hang in, and keep listening to what was going on. Even when hanging in was possibly hurtful to you, and our hearts were going out to you, you would keep trying to understand what was happening for people.

Michael: You talked about Denise's accepting and understanding ways, and said that these were principles.

Katherine: Yeah. I would say they are principles. [turning to Denise] You would stand by these principles of understanding and acceptance. Even when we were worried about you getting hurt, you wouldn't budge in this. Whenever we managed to put our worrying aside, it was always somehow refreshing to see you doing this. It was different. Wouldn't you say so, Gordon?

Gordon: I agree with Katherine. I've seen this too, many times. Even when you were just a little kid, this acceptance and understanding meant a lot to your grandfather, who was losing his way through brain degeneration, and no one else had much patience for him.

Michael: Denise, what do you think of this? Do you relate to what your mom and dad are saying about these principles?

Denise: I haven't thought much about it.

Michael: Are you thinking about it now? Or are you thinking about something else?

Denise: I'm thinking about it. Let's see . . . Yeah, I think it is right.

Michael: In that case, so far I understand that you used your will-power to get free of some of these expectations, and that your principles of understanding and acceptance guided you in this. How does that sound to you?

Denise: Kinda good.

Michael: Why would you say "kinda good?"

Denise: Well, this makes me feel just a little bit better.

Michael: Would it be okay with you for us to talk about what your life looks like when this willpower is available to you, and when it is being guided by what is important to you?

Denise: Yeah. But Mom and Dad could help. Couldn't you? [glancing in parents' direction]

Katherine: Well, for a start, when this is all working for her, she is not harassed by time like the rest of us. And I know that people around her don't have to put on such a brave face about things in their own lives that are not working out. I have noticed that they can just let go a bit. They don't have to be so uptight. Maybe because Denise is accepting of other people's complications, of their quirks, they can be more accepting of them as well.

Gordon: It is like when things are working for Denise, she has this ability to provide a bit of a haven for others. I can think of quite a few people that I reckon have found this quite a relief.

Michael: A haven! Now that presents me with a powerful image. Denise, what pictures of your life are coming to you as you listen to your parents' words?

Denise: Nice ones. Well . . . they are a bit hard for me to talk about. But I do like them.

Michael: Do you think it would be helpful if these pictures stayed with you, and if you had more like these?

Denise: Yeah.

Michael: Why would you say this would be helpful?

Denise: These pictures might make me feel better about myself, and that would make a big difference.

Michael: What sort of difference?

Denise: I maybe wouldn't get so worried and upset.

Michael: You'd like to talk more about these pictures of your life? For us to draw them out more?

Denise: Yeah.

Katherine: I think this has been very affirming of Denise. And I have been having lots of realizations as well. These are going to help, particularly with the sense of failure. I mean to help get free of this. For all of us.

Michael: Gordon?

Gordon: Yeah. I think that we should talk more about this. You know, when you think about it, when you really sit back and think about it, you realize our daughter really is an original. She really is! And for her to know this more, well, that would be fantastic.

Katherine, Gordon, Denise, and Michael: [all profoundly and visibly moved by this wonderful description of one of Denise's central attributes—"an original"]

Michael: An original! That is really something!

I met with Denise, Katherine, and Gordon on eight further occasions over a twelve-month period, and then twelve months later for three more occasions. The conversations we had in these meetings contributed to a rich description of the:

1. principles that guided Denise's expressions of willpower
2. ways of being in the world that didn't conform to everyone else's expectations, and for which Denise became a champion
3. skills of living that were associated with these ways of being in the world
4. unique aspirations that Denise had for her life: no longer for a "normal" life, no longer for a "productive" life, but for what Gordon described in our third meeting as a "life of honor."

Over this time, Denise became generally less stressed, felt more pride, and less vulnerable to the sort of insecurity that would make her prey to the hostile voices (auditory hallucinations) that had been so unsettling to her in the past. With this improvement in her quality of life, she became more socially adventurous. Hopelessness was displaced by a sense of her life unfolding.

As an outcome of these meetings, Gordon and Katherine also reported significant progress in regard to the lowering of their general stress levels. They both experienced a "steadiness" in themselves that had been elusive, felt less vulnerable to the opinions and expectations of others, and said that they were no longer on "tenterhooks for seventy percent of the time." They were more able to take upsets in stride and had become less inclined to "double guess" the responses of others to their words and actions.

Denise, with the help of her parents, found a way to escape failure. She abandoned the goals of productivity, and independence. She no longer exhausted herself trying to fit her life into the mainstream expectations of our culture, and in doing so, she stepped away from the sense that she was a spectacular failure as a person. In fact, in the shadows of failure there was achievement. Denise came to realize that she stood for something—being an "original." And she came to see that she was seeking a "life of honor."

The Bigger Picture

In any culture, there is a dominant belief system or "story" about what it means to be a worthy person. In Western culture, at this time in history, this belief system emphasizes being self-possessed and self-contained and having a productive and useful life. It values individuality at the expense of community, independence at the expense of connection. These are culturally specific values, but they are presented to us as "universal," "healthy," "human" attributes to strive for.

Some of us do reasonably well at conforming to these cultural norms. We get to be quite good at giving others the impression that we are pretty much together, that we are relatively independent, and that we have mostly made it in terms of leading a productive life. Because of our ability to successfully project this image to others, people include us as "normal," and this contributes to our feeling that we are of value.

But this is not always a simple achievement. In our efforts to conform to what it means to be a "real person" in today's culture, we are encouraged to keep rating and measuring ourselves against so many standards and norms. We can rate ourselves on how normal or abnormal we are, how healthy or unhealthy, how adequate or inadequate, how competent or incompetent, and so on. We can also try to measure our degree of independence. In modern times, there are more and more of these tables and continuums that we measure ourselves and each other against. This is why the phenomenon of personal failure has grown so rapidly over recent decades, and this is why there are so many more opportunities now to experience ourselves as failures.

We all have moments in which we find ourselves on the wrong end of these continuums, or uncomfortably close to the bottom of one of these tables of performance! And in response to finding ourselves at the wrong end of these continuums, many of us work hard to bring our lives into harmony with what is expected or seen to be desirable. As Denise described, this quest can become exhausting.

There are so many cultural expectations to measure ourselves against. Consider the following list, and as you do so, you might like to make a note of the expectations that you measure yourself against and those that you do not (or that you used to but no longer do). If there are some extras that you want to add, there is room to do so at the bottom of the table.

Expectation	Yes	No (longer)
1. To keep it together at all times		
2 To be independent in all aspects of life		
3. To be able to handle myself confidently in all social situations		

Expectation	Yes	No (longer)
4. To have a career path and trajectory		
5. To climb the corporate ladder		
6. To reproduce (to have children)		
7. To be in a long-term sexual relationship		
8. To find happiness in an exclusive sexual relationship with one other person		
9. To be wealthy		
10. To do as well as or better in life (whatever that means) than my neighbors/friends/ colleagues/schoolmates		
11. To always be in control of my emotions		
12. To be productive; to produce things		
13. To fulfill my goals for my life on a well-defined schedule		
14. To judge myself against how others are doing in their lives		
15. To have a six-pack abdomen		
16. To be successful at work		
17. To have hair that is always tidy		
18. To own possessions—especially my own house and car		
19. To know exactly where I am going in life		
20. To be able to perform under pressure		
21. To be able to balance a career, relationships, family, keeping fit and healthy, caring for elderly parents, keeping the garden watered —all with a smile on my face		
22. To be on time		
23. To be comfortable speaking in public		
24. To be the best lover my partner has ever had		
25. To keep my home and office clean and orderly		
26. To do my taxes when they're due		
27. To put others first		
28. To have 190 Facebook friends (or more)		
29. To find a knight in shining armor or glamorous princess (or be a knight in shining armor or glamorous princess!)		

Trying to live a life driven by these sorts of expectations can be exhausting. Particularly when you consider that these do not include ethical and moral concerns like:

- Not hurting others
- Honoring those who have been good to us
- Being a good friend
    . . . and so on.

Extraordinary Lives

There is, however, a way out of this exhaustion. Let's again turn to those who have had to develop special knowledge about sidestepping normality and honoring diverse ways of living–those who have experienced significant mental health struggles and those who live with disabilities. Some years ago, I attended a narrative gathering of people with mental health struggles.[3] My role was to document what was spoken during this significant event in words and in song. During the gathering, participants considered the following questions:

- Are there things that you value now, or that you think are precious, because you have lived a different sort of life?
- When you think about the life you aspire to these days; what would you call it? How have you learned that this is the sort of life you are seeking?
- Are there skills you have developed in living a different sort of life that you take a degree of pride in? What are they? How did you develop these skills? How do you put them to use in your daily life?

The group became excited and curious about transcending the taken-for-granted ways of living and thinking in our society. In fact, this became a bit of an adventure. We were questioning together and investigating what we each stood for in life. And we discovered that beyond any notion of conformity or normality, each of us stood for certain values. Each of us had particular ideas about what it means to live an ethical or good life. Each of us wanted to live our life in solidarity with certain key principles. One phrase in particular seemed to inspire us: "These are not ordinary lives we are living." Here are some of the responses and stories that people shared.

These Are Not Ordinary Lives We Are Living

Many of us have lived lives outside the ordinary. While some of our different experiences have been very difficult, we have also come to embrace some aspects of this difference. We have questioned a lot about life and have come to some interesting conclusions. We have come to value certain things that once we may not have valued. We have different aspirations these days, different ideas about what is a successful life.

We have developed different visions about what we want out of life and what we believe is important. Some of us have become good listeners. We support each other and have developed a good understanding of mental health issues. Some of us have learned how to be very flexible and make allowances for others. Some of us now cherish living a nonjudgmental life. Others of us have become advocates for people with mental health issues. Some of us have a commitment to human rights and political activism and have been involved in anti-racism campaigns over the years. These are all things in which we take a certain pride.

What's more, where once we may have been misfits, we have found company in being in a group of misfits. We celebrate each other's achievements. We love seeing others take small steps. In seeing someone do her own washing up—do it for herself rather than having it done for her. These moments can be a cause for celebration. We are more conscious now of honoring the little, but important, moments of life.

Relationships

My values have certainly changed. I have learned to place a much greater importance on relationships. When I was young, I was concerned with notions of success in conventional terms: study, university, getting a successful job. While all of this can be important in context, there's no point in pursuing these goals if the pursuit leaves you isolated from others and not being true to your own values. Now there is nothing more important to me than relationships with friends whom I love and who love me. They sustain me. Once I thought that being an adult was about being a lone wolf, battling through, trying to prove that I could do it on my own. Now, though, I am much happier being a part of a community of mutual support. We acknowledge that we couldn't do it without each other.

Honesty

My illness has actually resulted in me living a more honest life. I am more deliberate in whom I choose to open up to. The people I connect with are those with whom I have positive interactions. And I am now only interested in genuine friendships. I used to put up with friendships that were superficial, but I do not have the energy or the interest for this anymore. I am more selective and I live a more honest life. I treasure this and respect it.

Small Things

I notice the colors of the sky, of the leaves, and of artwork. I rely on little things to sustain me now and have stopped waiting for big things to change my life. My kids asked me once why I was happy despite all of the terrible things that were going on in my life, and I said that there are still so many precious things available to me. I love the smell of tomato seeds between my fingers. I love my four-year-old grandson, who said I was lovely and soft and squishy. I love the hairs on the nape of his neck. These small things are what have become important to me.

Independence

I value my independence. I was kicked out of home some time ago, so I moved around and eventually got things together. Six months ago I got a new place to live. Now I wash my own clothes, make my own meals. I treasure this and value sanity more than ever.

Pursuing Certain Paths in Life

Through these experiences I have gained more clarity about certain paths that I want to be on in life. These are not paths that I always manage to stay on, but they are paths I want to keep returning to. The path that is most significant to me these days is one of "principled love." I want to live my life according to this ethic.

Letting Go

I have let go of chasing careers and success. What is important to me now are friends, cooking a meal, washing, and coffee with friends. I have set myself free from the treadmill. I am now much more interested in spending time in peaceful, quiet places.

Living in the Present Moment
Some of us have learned to live one day at a time, to stop looking toward the future. We place a new value on what we have and what happens each day. Having a coffee with a friend, taking a shower—these become experiences to value and appreciate rather than a blur in a rush toward tomorrow. I'm studying at university right now, and when people ask me when I will be finished, I simply say, "I don't know." This is just what I am doing now.

During the gathering, we also wrote a song. Here are its lyrics:

These Are Not Ordinary Lives

With each other we find safety

Places free of pressure

No need to perform

Reaching out, even through our pain

It's connection that brings beauty to the day

And when we're at our lowest

Might be a pet who sees us through

Might be a sister or a friend

Who offers company through the blues

We've learned what works, what heals

What makes a soothing place

We've learned when to walk away

And if that doesn't work

Well bloodymindedness might just be the way

These are not ordinary lives

That we're living

There are sparkling moments in which we take pride

Hard-won skills we've developed

And we know what it means to be kind

Resigning from Normality

Some people are now resigning from normality and unin- vited expectations and instead turning their energy toward acts of care for themselves, for others, and for the world.

Harry, for instance, consulted Michael White after a long history of experiencing himself as a total failure as a person.[4] Harry had a well-established and acknowledged psychiatric career, which included a number of hospital admissions fol- lowing a series of what are commonly referred to as acute episodes. Harry had also collected several diagnoses, from schizophrenia to manic depressive illness. But then, Harry took a significant step, as Michael White (1994) describes:

> In Harry's attempts to achieve a sense of moral worth in his community, he had been policing his thoughts, his body, his lifestyle, his soul, and so on. He had been doing all of this in

the name of self-possession, self-containment, self-dependence, and so on—nothing special, you know, just the sort of specifications for personhood that are valorized in our culture. Well, he quit. He suddenly resigned from all this, and instead began to respect and honor his protest to all of these requirements. As an outcome of this, all of those ambitions and expectations that were stretching him and stressing him, and contributing to a vulnerability to "acute episodes," were suddenly thrown overboard, without any apology, without any excuses. It was a glorious moment, and together we laughed so much that we cried. I felt so privileged to be part of this. As an outcome of this, for the first time in Harry's memory, he experienced his life going forward in positive ways and found the state of mind that he had been searching for over such a long time: "calm sensibleness." After a time, Harry was ready to take certain steps to introduce others in his community to his achievement, and to enlist them in his project. He believed that this would discourage others from subjecting him to inappropriate expectations, further reduce the stresses in his life, and contribute further to his quality of life. I suggested that he might best achieve this by a statement that gave details of his project and extended to others an invitation to join him in it. So, after I asked Harry a series of questions, we put together the following document:

Expectations and My Life

1. I've learned a lot about expectations and what they demand of people.
2. Expectations can have a very destructive effect on my life and on the lives of other people.

3. Expectations have me feeling bad about myself and pressuring myself in unhelpful ways.
4. If you want to help me in my life, then please don't pressure me and don't expect me to be someone else who you want me to be. This includes expectations about health—I won't be guilt's person.
5. If you would like, I will provide you with a further and fuller understanding about the effects of expectations on my life and about what expectations have done to my life in the past.
6. Thank you for your time.

Harry distributed thirty signed copies of this document to key people in his life and was successful in his efforts to engage others in extending his chosen lifestyle of "calm sensibleness."

Exchanging Expectations of Normality with Acts of Solidarity

There is another significant aspect of resigning from normality that is significant to mention. It is perhaps summed up by a saying of my father's that echoes in my mind:

"Life's too short to care about what the mainstream dictates, when there's a world to save and breakthroughs to make."

The "normal" world is one of gross injustices. It is a place of profound everyday violence in so many family homes. The "normal" form of economics has led to devastation of the world's environments. "Normal" gender and sexual relations remain unjust to women, and to lesbian, gay, bisexual, queer, trans, and intersex folks. There are many aspects of normal, mainstream culture that we may wish to separate ourselves from because we believe they are unjust.

Figure 6.1. My father, Dr. Michael Denborough, being escorted by police away from a protest outside an international weapons trade fair.

At this point, inspired by Denise and Harry, you might like to write down three expectations of normality that you (or you and a friend) are going to resign from.

1.
2.
3.

Now, with the energy and time made available to you from these resignations, write down three acts of solidarity that you will prioritize instead. Acts of solidarity include acts of justice or actions of care toward yourself, others, or the natural world.

1.
2.
3.

A Checklist

With a touch of irony, this chapter ends with a checklist or questionnaire.[5] As I mentioned earlier, these days there are so many ways that we can rate ourselves to see if we fit in with what's "normal." In so many popular magazines, we can fill out questionnaires and rate ourselves in relation to our sex lives, fitness regimes, lifestyles, and so on. Well, in humorous defiance, here is an alternative questionnaire to see how we are doing at questioning normality and escaping failure.

This checklist can be done individually or with others. You might even like to share it with a friend for whom you think it might be helpful.

Escaping from Failure and Questioning Normality Checklist

Place a check mark in the right-hand column for each category you achieve in your life (or have achieved in the past).   **Yes**

---

1 Make simple mistakes and errors of everyday life in the context of social relations that are considered to reflect a lack of togetherness or social competence

2 Fail to achieve desired ends in regard to personal development objectives (and change your objectives along the way)

3 Go off track in terms of your goals for your life (and find yourself unexpectedly on another track)

4 Experience apprehension while on your path to true confidence

6 Experience a glitch in relation to your efforts to be who you truly are

7 Let options for self-cultivation slip past unnoticed

8 Unknowingly forego opportunities to realize your full potential

---

(Continued)

Escaping from Failure and Questioning Normality Checklist

Place a check mark in the right-hand column for each
category you achieve in your life (or have achieved in
the past).   **Yes**

9   Neglect to seize upon opportunities that are available to you to
    engage in judging yourself and/or others as to whether you/they
    are fulfilling "normal"/"proper" ways of living

10 Overlook chances to rank yourself and/or others on this or that
    table of performance or on continuums of development, health,
    and normality

11 Obstinately reject aspirations for the achievement of superior
    status

12 Willfully resist the classification of people's lives

13 Show an interest in forms of relationship that are beyond the
    mainstream heterosexual couple relationship/nuclear family
    (this could include an interest in loyalty to imaginary friends,
    concern for the earth and all living things, valuing friendship
    equally with romantic ties, valuing diverse forms of family, and
    so on)

14 Take an interest in how ideas of what is normal vary across
    cultures, across class, between genders, across history

15 Revel in some of the unusual ways in which others (friends,
    family members, or people in the present or past whom you
    admire) live life outside the "norm"

16 Encourage others to pursue lives that fit them rather than
    mainstream expectations (as long as they are not harming others)

17 Act with kindness and/or solidarity to others when you know
    they are experiencing a sense of failure to conform to mainstream
    "standards"

Escaping from Failure and Questioning Normality Checklist

Place a check mark in the right-hand column for each category you achieve in your life (or have achieved in the past).	Yes
18 Value acts of justice and ethics of care (for oneself, others, and the earth) over and above expectations of "normality"	
19 Defiantly resist filling out questionnaires even if they are about escaping from normality	

Now for the fun part. Add up the number of check marks in the right-hand column. Add ten. If the total is now ten or more, congratulations! You are now eligible for the following certificate:

Escaping from Failure and Questioning Normality Certificate

This certificate is awarded to _____.

for

- Deciding not to measure their life against other people's measurements of success
- Using the energy that would have gone into chasing normality for acts of kindness, solidarity, care, and justice

"Life's too short to care about what the mainstream dictates when there's a world to save and breakthroughs to make."

Having written your name in the above certificate (or the name of your friend, sibling, colleague, child, etc., if you are facilitating this process with them), you might like to arrange an award ceremony. You may or may not choose to have other people, pets, or favorite music present. Invite (literally or figuratively) whomever you think would be least surprised and most supportive of your efforts to escape from normality. You can sign the certificate yourself, or you may insert the paw print or signature of someone else. Alternatively, please feel free to insert my father's name, Michael Antony Denborough. I can assure you, he would be cheering "Bravo" at your award ceremony if he could be present.

Studying Our Own Culture

If we start to question normality, it's like becoming an anthropologist in our own lives. Here's an exercise that can assist us to study our own culture. By yourself, or with a friend, take a piece of paper and draw two lines so that the paper is divided into three columns. Carry a pen or pencil and this piece of paper with you for one week.

In the left-hand column, jot down every time you hear, watch, or read an opinion, judgment, conclusion, attitude, viewpoint, inference, evaluation, or taken-for-granted assumption about what life is all about. Jot down every time you hear someone professing to know what the truth of life (or some aspect of life) is all about for others.

In the middle column, jot down every time you *could* have made such an opinion, judgment, conclusion, attitude, viewpoint, inference, evaluation, or taken-for-granted assumption about what would be good for someone else's life, but didn't.

In the right-hand column, jot down every time you notice yourself or others engaging in acts of solidarity, acts of justice, or acts of care for themselves, others, or the world, that might not be highly valued by the mainstream culture of "success" but that will contribute to the world being a better place for someone (human or nonhuman) to live in.

This exercise can assist us to begin to notice how common it is for people to claim what is right, what is normal, and what is healthy for others. And gradually, we can realize how significant it can be to refrain from making such judgments about other people's lives. Life can start to look far more interesting when we question normality and embrace diverse ways of living.

Looking Back, Looking Forward

In this chapter, we have taken the significant step of questioning normality. In doing so, we have the chance to free ourselves from the constraints of mainstream expectations—expectations that all too often set us up for failure. In questioning our own culture, we have the opportunity to exchange mainstream expectations for acts of solidarity. We have the opportunity to shape the direction of our own lives according to what we value and care about.

This can be particularly important if we have endured traumatic experience, which is the topic of the next chapter.

Notes

1. The story of Denise and her parents was first published in White, 2002b.
2. An example of such a master list of expectations can be found on pp. 157–158.
3. For more information about this gathering, see ACT Mental Health Consumers Network & Dulwich Centre, 2003.

4. The story of Harry was originally told by Michael White (1994) in an interview with Donald Bubenzer, John West, and Shelly Boughner.

5. The questionnaire includes ideas from Michael White's writings (White, 2002b).

CHAPTER 7

Reclaiming Our Lives from Trauma and Honoring What Is Precious to Us

THIS CHAPTER CONSIDERS ways of reclaiming our lives from trauma. In particular, it honors those special skills and the personal qualities that make it possible for people to survive traumatic experiences. In the following pages, I will *not* invite or encourage you to revisit the original traumatic experience as a way of breaking free of it.[1] Instead, let us explore those survival skills that make it possible for people to "navigate through the dark hours of their lives and into the present" (White, 1995a, p. 85).

No child or adult is a passive recipient of trauma, regardless of the nature of this trauma. People always respond in some way. Among other things, people take action to minimize their exposure to trauma and to decrease their vulnerability to it. However, it is rare for people's responses to the traumas of their lives to ever be acknowledged. It is more common for these responses to go unnoticed, or to be punished, ridiculed, and diminished within the trauma context. This makes it less likely that people will remember how they responded. The actions they took to try to minimize harm to themselves or others become forgotten, invisible, erased.

So it can be necessary for us to help one another to acknowledge the special skills and the personal qualities that made it possible for us to navigate through the dark hours of life into the present. To demonstrate this, Michael White recounts his conversations with a boy named Paul in which they discovered how he had navigated devastating schoolyard abuse (White, 2004b, pp. 56–58).

Paul, a twelve-year-old boy, was brought to see me by his mother and father, who were highly concerned about him. According to them, he was persistently sad, apprehensive, and lonely, and in a variety of ways he had been expressing highly negative thoughts about his identity and about his life. As the parents described their concerns to me, Paul cried silently. According to the parents, Paul had always been a sensitive boy who had a habit of taking things to heart. It hadn't been uncommon for him to be distressed about many of the trials and tribulations of his childhood, but over the past eighteen months his parents had noticed the development of a more general apprehensiveness and sadness that was now touching virtually every aspect of his existence.

Paul was still crying, so I asked his parents some questions about what they understood to be the context of this development. Among other things, Paul's mother spoke of the incessant teasing and bullying that he had been subject to at school recently. At this juncture, Paul began to sob, and I took this to be confirmation of his mother's observation about the significance of this teasing and bullying.

I turned to consult Paul about this, but he made it clear that he wasn't yet ready to join our conversation. I asked him if it

*would be okay for me to interview his parents about their fur-
ther understanding of this teasing and its effects on his life,
and he signaled that this would be okay. I then initiated a
conversation with the parents regarding what they knew
about the specific tactics of this teasing and the attitudes that
were expressed, and regarding what they understood to be the
consequences of this in Paul's life.*

*For example, I inquired about their understanding of how
these tactics and attitudes were affecting Paul's image of
himself as a person, and about what they were talking him
into about his life. I also inquired about their understanding of how these tactics were interfering with his social and
emotional worlds. It seemed quite clear that these were isolating Paul and highly disturbing his emotional life. It was
at this point that, for the first time, his mother declared that
it was "abuse" that Paul was being subjected to. Paul now
seemed more ready to enter the conversation. In response to
my inquiry, he confirmed his parents' speculation about his
sadness and loneliness, and about the negative conclusions
that he held about his identity and his life: that he was
"weak," "pathetic," "inadequate" and "incompetent." He also
confirmed their understandings about the principal context
of these experiences—incessant teasing and frequent bullying
at school. I was openly curious about how Paul had been
able to enter our conversation. I wondered aloud whether it
was his parents' naming of the tactics of peer abuse, the
naming of the attitudes expressed in these tactics, or their
understandings of the consequences of these to his life that
had something to do with this. Paul confirmed that it was
all of these, and as our conversation developed I learned*

that this was the first occasion upon which these tactics and attitudes and their consequences had been named in their particularities. It was clear that this had provided him with some relief.

When I initiated a conversation about the action that the family had taken in their efforts to address these circumstances, I learned that Paul's mother had endeavored to take the problem up with school authorities on several occasions, but to no avail. Each time her concerns had been dismissed with versions of, "We have looked into this, and believe that the problem resides principally with Paul. He clearly needs some assistance with his self-esteem," and "Don't you think it's about time that Paul looked at himself? It's a big world out there, and he's just going to have to learn to be more assertive."

I initiated an inquiry into Paul's responses to what he was being subjected to. As an outcome of this inquiry, we discovered that, among other things, he had taken steps to befriend the school librarian so that he could spend lunchtime in the school library, away from the culture of the schoolyard. This and other initiatives were unpacked in our conversation. As an upshot of this, Paul and his parents became much more familiar with the initiatives that Paul had been developing, with the roots of these, and with what these initiatives reflected about what he accorded value to in life. It was readily apparent that Paul was finding further comfort in this evolving conversation in which the particularities of his responses to trauma were becoming more richly known.

With the approval of Paul and his parents, I called the school. It was my hope that some collaboration with the relevant school authorities might contribute to general initiatives in addressing those aspects of the culture of the schoolyard that were abusive, and to specific initiatives in response to Paul's experience of this abuse. I had also hoped that it would be possible for me to meet with the children who were perpetrating the peer abuse. The school's response to my overture confirmed the prediction of Paul's mother—it was not positive. Despite the care that I took, the school principal was clearly annoyed with my approach and demanded to know, "What are these allegations about the culture of the schoolyard?"

I called Paul's family and spoke to his mother about a substitute plan—to invite to our next meeting other children, strangers to Paul, who had insider experience of peer abuse. I suggested that these children might appreciate aspects of Paul's story that might be lost to us as adults, and that their responses might provide Paul with the sort of validation that was beyond our ability to provide. Paul's mother was enthusiastic about this idea, as, apart from other things, Paul's acute loneliness had been such a source of concern to her. Paul's father's response was, "Well, I guess we've got nothing to lose!" Paul felt positive about the idea, although he was somewhat apprehensive about it.

In the context of therapeutic practice, it is not uncommon for me to refer to my registers—lists of names and contact details of people who have consulted me in the past and who have volunteered to contribute to my work with people who follow in their footsteps. So, from my register of the names of children who had been referred to me in relation to the consequences of peer abuse in their lives, I called the families of the three most recent volunteers. I did not need to proceed up the list, as all of these children were enthusiastic about this summons, as were their parents. Before long I was meeting with Paul, his parents, and these three guests.

At the outset of this meeting, I interviewed Paul about his experiences of peer abuse, about what he had learned about the specific tactics of peer abuse that he had been subjected to, about the consequences of this in his life, and about his responses to what he had been put through. I scaffolded the conversation so as to provide Paul with an opportunity to vividly describe the initiatives that he had engaged in and relate what it was that he had continued to give value to in his life and had refused to surrender. During this first part of our meeting, our three guests were strictly an audience to our conversation.

I then asked Paul and his parents to sit back and began to interview the children about:

1. *what they had heard from Paul that had particularly captured their attention;*
2. *the mental pictures and metaphors that this had evoked, and what these suggested to them about who Paul was as a person and about what was important to him;*
3. *why they could relate to what they were hearing; what this struck a chord with in their own experience; and*
4. *where they had personally journeyed on account of being present as witnesses to Paul's story about the abuse he had been subjected to and his responses to it.*

It was in the context of this retelling that what Paul stood for in life became more richly known: "Paul didn't let himself get caught up in all of this. Nothing that these kids did could get him to join in with them in this teasing and bullying"; "Paul stands for more caring and understanding ways"; "Paul is one of those kids who won't pass the buck. He didn't find smaller kids to pass this bullying on to." As the retelling of these three children evolved, Paul began to cry, and then to sob. It was my guess that this was because the very ways of being in life that had been so demeaned and disqualified in the context of peer abuse were now being acknowledged and honored. It was also my guess that, on account of this, Paul was separating from all of the negative conclusions that had been imposed on his identity in the context of peer abuse. When it came time for our three witnesses to sit back and for me to interview Paul about what he had heard in this retelling, he confirmed my hunch. The experience of this retelling did turn out to be a turning point in his life, and I gained a strong sense that he would never again be vulnerable to these negative conclusions about his identity and his life.

There is more to the story of my conversations with Paul, his parents, and the three children who joined as witnesses for three of these conversations. I will just say a little of one of the developments that unfolded during the course of our meetings, and that I considered to be outstanding. I learned in my fifth meeting that Paul had begun to make it his business to seek out other children who had insider knowledge of peer abuse. Most of these children were from his school. Upon identifying these children, he would engage them in conversations about how being subject to peer abuse reflected what was important to them and what they stood for in life—that is, more honorable ways of being boys in the culture of the schoolyard. Also, because the identification and appreciation of his own responses to peer abuse had been very significant for Paul, he *would invite these other children to relate stories about their responses to what they had been put through. This was contributing to the development of an alternative culture of the schoolyard. At a subsequent meeting, I had the great pleasure of meeting with Paul and several of these children.*

How we respond during times of trauma, and how we protect ourselves and others, provides clues about what we care about in life. Our responses are based on what we give value to. Once Paul's responses became known and acknowledged, they indicated what he stood for in life—not passing the buck, not passing on peer abuse, and finding more honorable ways to be a boy.

In Michael's conversations with Paul, his parents, and the other children, Paul's *responses* to trauma were made visible, and everyone came to know and acknowledge what was important to him. This freed Paul from some of the very negative ideas he had come to think about himself. There was another significant step in this process. When Paul got to hear from the other children about what his story had meant to them and how it might lead them to take further action to redress the injustices of peer abuse, he came to realize that what he had been through was not for nothing. He could make a contribution to the lives of others who were also suffering from peer abuse. Finding ways to use hard-won knowledge to contribute to the lives of others in hardship can bring healing from trauma.

Noticing the Responses of Children

Angel Yuen is a Canadian therapist who works with children and young people, many of whom have been through traumatic experiences.[2] In her conversations with them, she asks them various questions to try to learn about the actions they took to endure some of their hard times. These questions include:

- How did you respond? What did you do?
- What did you do when you were scared?
- What did you show/not show on your face during times of abuse?
- Where did you hide when you were scared?
- What did you do once you found a place to hide?
- Even though it was not possible for you to stop the violence as a child, how did you attempt to protect yourself and/or others?
- How did you comfort yourself and/or your siblings?
- How did your brothers and sisters comfort you?
- What did you do/are you doing to lessen the effects of abuse (or witnessing violence, the death of your parent, etc.)?

Angel describes some of the responses she has heard from children (Yuen, 2007, p.7):

When I ask about the places of safety that children have found during times of immense fear, children bring forth many images of their creative responses and are therefore less likely to feel like a passive recipient to trauma. Michael, a seven-year-old boy who faced emotional abuse that he described as "the bad, angry, and scary voice," would often hide from place to place in his house in attempts to "get away" from the harsh voice. His hiding place of choice was a closet that was never used. By simply asking where Michael hid, he became more in touch with what else was happening at the time and how he responded. When I asked him, "So when you hid in the closet, what did you do to comfort yourself once you were safe?" he replied, "I would sing a song to myself, and that would make the tears go away."

When Megan, a sixteen-year-old girl who described herself to me as "messed up," told me about the difficult times of her life, I wondered about the ways she had kept herself safe when her mother would pass out from high alcohol use. She replied, "I think I was about six years old, and I remember being so afraid that intruders would come in while my mom was passed out. Sometimes drug dealers would come. So I would hide. There was this old mattress that was tucked underneath a bed, and I would wiggle in between the mattress and hide under the bed."

I asked Megan how long she would be under the bed, and she remembered that it was sometimes up to eight hours at a time. I asked her, "What did you do all of those hours underneath the bed? That's a long time to be hiding. I know it was ten years ago, but do you remember yourself as a little girl and what you did or what you thought about while hiding?" Megan thoughtfully said, "Hmmm . . . this sounds funny . . . but I used something sharp to carve things in the board above my head while I was lying underneath there all that time. I would carve x's and hearts. I would put the initials of people that I knew I wasn't safe with beside the x's, and I would carve the initials of people that I knew cared for me inside of the hearts. Then I would think about my mom eventually waking up and how I would help her to feel better and take care of her. And then I guess at some point I fell asleep."

Adults Looking Back

It can be equally significant when we, as adults, look back on certain events from our earlier years with a focus on our *responses* to traumatic experiences. Jussey Verco (2002, pp. 25–26) describes some of the conversations she shares with adult women* who are survivors of childhood sexual abuse:

> Survivors of childhood sexual abuse have often been recruited into believing that they were somehow responsible for the abuse they experienced. This is a potent recipe for self-hate and self-loathing. This experience can be better understood when located within broader cultural practices. Patriarchal culture commonly locates women as the center of problems in families. Blame is laid at women's feet in relation to most family issues. This means that, in working with survivors, we are often engaged in conversations to free women from the grips of self-blame. In some ways, this can be seen as a process of self-forgiveness.
>
> There are a number of factors of critical importance in this process. First of all, the women need to be believed and to have their experiences honored and respected. I can't emphasize enough how significant this is. Just about every woman with whom I have worked was not believed when she first disclosed her experiences of abuse. This initial disbelief often has a significant impact on a woman's sense of self-worth. When a child not only is subject to abuse, but is then not believed about this abuse, their sense of identity and their sense of entitlement to respect and care can be greatly diminished.
>
> The second crucial factor relates to honoring the acts of resistance in which these women engaged when they were children. We seek to create a context in which women can begin to tell and retell the stories of how as children they sought safety, or how they resisted, or how they ran away. While

---

* These considerations are also relevant for men who have experienced childhood sexual abuse.[3]

relating these stories can at first be difficult for survivors, when the stories begin to be told and acknowledged, women start to get a different sense of themselves. They begin to see themselves in a different light. No longer do they see themselves as a person who was solely victimized by the abuse, or as a person who in some way colluded with the abuse. Instead they begin to acknowledge that as children they actively tried, in the ways available to them, to resist what they were being subjected to.

These stories need not be grand stories of resistance. For instance, they might consist of the times when she climbed the tallest tree in the backyard and stayed there until she was forced to come down. They might be stories of the times when she sat on the back fence for hours upon hours; or when she climbed to the roof; or ran away; or used her imagination to climb through the cracks in the wall. Or they might be stories about how she used to disassociate while her body was being subjected to sexual abuse so that her spirit wasn't present. When women begin to retell these stories and they are acknowledged as containing survival skills and knowledges, it can make a profound difference in how they understand themselves. Realizing that they engaged in some process of trying to keep themselves safe can enable women to contemplate what might be called "self-forgiveness." They are able to acknowledge that they did not agree to the abuse and that they really did try to stop it or to seek help.

Sharing these stories with an audience of other women survivors can also be transformative. This seems especially true for women who have previously understood their survival strategies in negative ways. For instance, many women who dissociated at the time of abuse have had concerns that this reflects that they were somehow "crazy" or "messed up." When they hear from other women who did the same thing, who honor the child's ability to care for herself, and who understand this as a survival strategy, it can be very liberating.

I recall one particular woman who, when we first started a conversation in the group about survival knowledges, said, "I didn't do anything." When we began to talk together about things that she had found hard as a child, she told us that she had been a tomboy. There were about twelve women present in the group that day, and as we went around the table, every single woman replied that she too had been a tomboy. Of course, we then had a discussion about what this could possibly mean, and the women came up with some fantastic reflections. Perhaps it meant that even as little girls they had thought that boys might be less likely to be subjected to sexual abuse. Or perhaps they had cut their hair and worn boys' clothes in order to appear less conventionally attractive. Or perhaps they had thought that if they hung out with the boys and something untoward began to happen, then the boys might keep them safe. Or perhaps they'd worked out that boys simply had more fun! One woman reflected on how the games that boys played, such as riding bikes, were much more appealing to her than the games the girls played, such as "mommies and daddies." This particular woman stated that she would have found it terrifying to play a game in which you were supposed to enact what mommies and daddies did. As women shared these experiences, there was an amazing ripple around the table as they recognized their childhood acts of resistance.

As women speak about their childhood acts of resistance and ways that they endeavored to either keep themselves safe or make some stand against what was happening, it takes away the power of "self-blame." The woman who at the beginning of the meeting had said that she hadn't done anything to resist came back the next week and said, "I've been smiling all week long knowing that, yes, I did, I really did try to make some kind of stand."

Sometimes survivors join groups to have a chance to share experiences of what they have endured and how they have endured it. The group of women survivors of childhood sexual abuse that Jussey Verco just described is called Silent Too Long. Here is what some of the members have said about their responses to the abuse they experienced:[4]

Honoring the Stands That We Took as Children to Protect Ourselves and Others

It's been important to me to acknowledge the stands that I took as a child to protect myself—like refusing to be left alone in the house with Uncle Bill or Grandad even if I was threatened with punishment for "being rude" or "not respecting my elders." There were also ways I protected others when I was small. When I was a kid, I didn't invite other kids to our house. I couldn't stand hearing and seeing what he did to them. Acknowledging the things we have done all our lives to protect ourselves and others can be significant and powerful for our own healing.

Honoring Our Acts of Resistance

After my father would rape and beat me, I would wait until he left the room. Then I would stand up. I would never let him totally win. There was a part of my inner being, my spirit, that would never agree with what was happening to me. I couldn't stand up while he was there—it would have been too dangerous. He would have beaten me again. But once it was safe, I stood up. There was a part of me he could never get to—my hope. I knew there were other ways of treating children, that this abuse was not justified—that it would never be. In retrospect, there were powerful choices and actions I made as an abused child, even if they seemed small and ineffectual at the time. Speaking about these acts of resistance and sharing them together has made a real difference.

Honoring the Ways in Which We Have Tried to Protect Others from Abuse

It's been important to us to acknowledge the acts we have taken to try to protect others—especially our children. There have been many examples, including: interviewing kindergarten teachers about their understandings of child protection; educating our doctors about child sexual abuse; educating other women in our lives; and calling upon the editor of the local newspaper to ensure responsible reporting of child abuse cases.

Turning Half-Memories into Full Memories: A Matter of Justice

Again, I'd like to emphasize that one's *responses* to traumatic experiences have usually been forgotten. Memories of responses to trauma are often erased because these responses were ridiculed and diminished, or because they were not recognized, confirmed, or acknowledged in a way that would contribute to their becoming familiar and honored. So often is this the case that Michael White used to refer to the process of drawing out and acknowledging people's responses to trauma as turning "half-memories" into "full memories."

This is also about justice. Honoring the responses of children and adults to trauma is often also about honoring responses to injustices. The steps a child takes to protect their younger sibling from an abusive adult deserve to be remembered—not only by the child but by our community. But if these responses are difficult to recall, what can we do?

First of all, we can recognize the diversity of people's responses to trauma. These can include, but are not limited to, ways in which children, young people, and adults:

- Act to preserve their lives in life-threatening contexts
- Find support in hostile environments
- Establish domains of safety in unsafe places
- Hold on to possibilities for life in circumstances that discourage hope
- Develop nurturing responses to others even in degrading situations
- Find connection with others in settings that are isolating
- Refuse to visit trauma on the lives of others
- Heal from the consequences of trauma under conditions that are unfavorable to healing
- Achieve degrees of self-acceptance in atmospheres that sponsor self-rejection

People's responses to trauma are often to be found in the small things that they do. It's the small steps that we are searching for—actions like feeding the cat, watering plants, making sure a brother or sister is clean and fed. Each of these actions or responses is also a clue to what the person gives value to—love, responsibility, care, duty, stability, and so on.

We can be on the lookout for these sorts of small but significant responses in the lives of those we know and care about. Do you know children, young people, or adults who are currently experiencing significant hardship or trauma? If so, take a moment to review the list above and see if you can identify any steps they are taking in their lives that could be understood as *responses* to trauma and that could be a testimony to what they value in life.

_____

_____

_____

_____

_____

If you have identified some of the actions the people in your life are taking to protect what is important to them, perhaps you can write them a short note acknowledging this. In this note, perhaps you can clearly state why their actions are significant to you, what their actions might inspire you to do in your life, and what small steps you might take as a result of that inspiration.

Your Own Life

You may also wish to acknowledge your own responses to traumatic experience and the ways you tried to protect what was important to you. One way of doing so is to write yourself a letter. Begin the letter as if you are writing to yourself. (For instance, I would write "Dear David.") In the first part of the letter, include a message to yourself at the time that you underwent trauma. What would you say to yourself if you had the chance?

Here are examples of messages that people who grew up with parents with significant mental health struggles would say to themselves as children:[5]

I would say, "It will be okay." As a child, I witnessed my mother's suffering and pain. The way that she coped (as I understand much later) with pain and depression was through the use of alcohol and sedatives. At the time when I was growing up, my life, as well as the life of my sister and family, was often marked by violence and abuse. At times, this invited hopelessness and fear about how life for my family and people that I loved would evolve. If I had heard something like, "It will be okay," I imagine it would have provided me with a sense of hope and comfort. It would also have been evidence that I was not alone.

• • •

I would say, "Your mother and father aren't well; that's why they are doing what they're doing. It's not your fault."

• • •

I would say, "There is a future, life is not always gonna be like this." Because when it was happening, I didn't even think of the future; it felt like it was going to be happening all the time.

• • •

I would say, "It wasn't about you." Why is this important? Having a mother take her own life had me wondering if she was unhappy because of me or my sister. Having a context for her actions (postpartum depression) helps me to separate what she did from the hopes and dreams she might have had for her life with us. This leaves space for a different mother-daughter story for me and my sister.

In the second part of your letter to yourself, acknowledge any of the responses that you made to the trauma and any of the ways in which you tried to protect what was important to you. These could include actions you took to preserve your life, find support, or establish safety in the physical world or in your mind; ways you held on to hope; steps you took to nurture or connect with others; ways in which you refused to traumatize others; or ways you found to achieve some sort of self-acceptance in the face of rejection.

Here's an example from a young woman looking back at how she coped as the child of parents with significant mental health struggles[6]:

Until I thought about what got me through those hard times, I hadn't "consciously" been aware that I drew on certain sustaining activities (outside of a few such as reading). In considering my survival skills I have generated the following list: Reading, nature, listening to music, singing, art and creating, roller-skating, BMX bike riding, swimming, dancing, other exercise, laughing with friends, the kindness of others, looking at the moon and the stars, standing in the rain, sharing love with animals, the kindness shown when parents weren't abusive, playing and imagining, noticing beauty, being hungry for knowledge and answers and finding things out, the capturing of insight, experiencing moments of transcendence, seeing and experiencing things in a way I'd never seen or felt before, finding sanctuary in being alone and withdrawing into the self, finding peace and quiet away from distractions, observing, just "being" without judgment, sleeping, exploring and having adventures, trying different roles—experimenting with identity, having meaningful conversations with others, being inspired by others, being independent, accepting support, looking after one's self, having a quiet joke with one's self, forgiving, being loved, doing things that make one feel proud of one's self.

I don't think that this list covers everything, and I think that everyone must have perhaps thousands of ways small and obscure, as well as extravagant, for coping during difficulty. Considering this has not only enabled me to bring into my conscious awareness the idea that I had ways of coping and to make me aware of what they were, but also to allow me to start to draw on them consciously as opposed to instinctually, which is what I had been doing. By doing so it also made me aware that I have the capacity within myself to find other ways of coping, perhaps more meaningful and effective ways.

Once you have included in your letter a message to yourself and an acknowledgment of any of your own responses to trauma, try to find words for what it was that you were protecting. Just as Paul stood for not passing the buck, not passing peer abuse on to others, and finding more honorable ways to be a boy, what do your responses to trauma indicate that you as a younger person stood for and believed in?

If you have typed your letter on a computer, print it out. Place it in an envelope and address it to yourself. Post it to your own address. When it arrives a few days later, honor its arrival. Take some time to create the most appropriate context in which to open it. Perhaps you can have a cup of tea, light a candle, or take the letter to the beach or to your garden. Decide whether you want to invite anyone to join you, or if you would prefer to conduct this ritual by yourself.

Once you open the letter, read it aloud to yourself. If you have any further thoughts or reflections, you can add these to the letter, or even write a second one. This is a process you can continue as many times as you wish.

You may not wish to share your letters with others. On the other hand, you may want to go through this writing process in collaboration with someone else. If so, there will be the opportunity to exchange letters and to convey how your collaborator's words and stories will contribute to your life and vice versa.

Escaping Adult Self-Abuse

There is another process that may be relevant if you were subject to emotional or physical abuse in childhood and adolescence. Sometimes people who were subjected to such abuse come to have a very negative and rejecting attitude toward themselves in adult life. This self-rejection is the result of taking on the abusing adult's attitude toward oneself. When this happens, it can be very difficult to rest. You may feel perpetually compelled to discipline yourself according to the abuser's attitudes.

If this is the case, sometimes it can be helpful to consider the following questions:[7]

- How do you imagine your life might have been if you'd had yourself as a father or mother?
- If you'd had yourself for a mother or father, what would you have appreciated about yourself as a child that wasn't appreciated in you as a child or adolescent?

- What difference would it have made to you growing up if you'd had yourself for a father or mother?
- In what ways would you have been more accepting of yourself?
- In what ways do you think that you might have experienced yourself as lovable?

Responding to these questions can contribute to forging a new relationship with oneself. Additionally, it can be intriguing to consider the following questions:

- In what ways do you think your father's or mother's life was richer for having known you as a child and adolescent?
- If your father or mother had been less blind to what there was to appreciate about you as a child and adolescent, and if they had been truly interested in acknowledging and experiencing this in you, what effect do you think this would have had on their quality of life?
- If you had yourself for a son or daughter, what potential would your interaction with this son or daughter have for enriching your life?

These questions make it possible for us to think differently about our lives as children. They invite us to identify personal qualities and characteristics we displayed as kids that might have been really appreciated by others under different circumstances. These questions also make it possible for people who have been abused to experience compassion for themselves that they often experience for others. Significantly, as adults, responding to these questions can dispossess parents who have been abusive from having the last say on matters of identity.

If you know someone who might be interested in considering these questions, you may like to share them with that person. Alternatively, you might like to take some time and write your own responses to them.

Creating a Nurturing Team

Having considered the importance of acknowledging the responses of children and adults to trauma and having explored ways of escaping adult self-abuse, let's now revisit the metaphor of teams that we considered in Chapter 4. Sometimes, in response to trauma, it makes a difference to take a team approach.[8]

We can sketch out and acknowledge two different teams. The first team can be called the "trauma team" or the "abuse team." Within this team we can include as members all those who were centrally and peripherally involved in causing the trauma, including those who were complicit with it even if they were not active in it. We may also include broader cultural considerations that contributed to the effects of the trauma. These might include cultural practices like disbelief or sexism or poverty or racism.

Now we can create a second team to provide a counterweight to the trauma or abuse team. The aim is for this "nurturing team" to eventually tip the balance in our favor. For this to happen, we need to include in this team as many people, figures, and positive cultural practices as we can. We may even need to do some calculations and projections to determine what sort of team and what sort of teamwork might be required. A well-trained, loyal, close-knit team can often overrun a more established team. So there are a lot of factors at play.

If you like the idea of forming a nurturing team, either for yourself or for someone you care about, it might be good to first enlist a coach who can help draft the invitations and facilitate the first team meeting. Someone who is experienced at working with teams and holding meetings is good for this role. It could be a friend, relative, community leader, or therapist.

Having enlisted a coach, there are a number of ways to develop nurturing teams.

1. It's possible to approach those you know and formally invite them to join the nurturing team.
2. Nurturing team membership can be increased by having the initial members suggest and approach others they think might be willing to join.
3. Pets are often significant members of nurturing teams.
4. Key positive figures from a person's past who may no longer be alive can be honorary members.
5. Associations that people belong to (for example, a church, temple, or mosque; a community organization; or a self-help group such as AA) may also be sources of membership.
6. People or organizations that are taking a stand against some of the cultural practices that support the "abuse team" (such as disbelief, sexism, poverty, or racism) can be enlisted as "sponsors."

Here is an example of an invitation letter:

Dear Sonya,

I hope you are well and that your exams went okay. I am writing with an unusual invitation.

As you know, I have been going through some hard times lately as a result of some pretty tough experiences that I went through a while back. It's taking me a while to get my life back on track. Over the last few months, you have been a really significant support to me. Your care and kindness have meant a lot.

I've been meeting with my aunt, and in talking together, we've had the idea of forming a "nurturing team" to help me get through the next few months until graduation. I'm writing now to invite you to be one member of this team.

If you're able to take me up on this invitation, we'll plan a team meeting to work out what people can and can't offer. My aunt has offered to help with the meeting.

Thank you for considering this, and for your friendship.

Love,

Amy

When prospective members receive formal invitations like this one, it is often reassuring to them that they will now be part of a team. It also helps if the nurturing work that the prospective team member has already contributed is acknowledged in the invitation letter. (Even when care is taken in issuing invitations, however, the person to whom it is addressed may still say no. It can be good to prepare for this possibility in advance.)

At the first nurturing team meeting, the person who has issued the invitations usually provides some account of the trauma team's membership, its activities, the duration of these activities, and the long-term effects of these activities. Second, the idea of the nurturing team is introduced, along with some thoughts about the part that this team could play in undoing the work of the trauma team. Third, the work that has *already* been done in this direction by prospective nurturing team members is acknowledged, along with the effects of this work. Fourth, prospective team members talk about the sort of ongoing contributions to nurturing work that they believe might challenge the work of the trauma team, and that might fit with the responsibilities of their own lives without being burdensome. Fifth, the person who called the meeting responds to these proposals and makes further suggestions about what might work best. Sixth, all of these proposals and suggestions are negotiated and detailed plans are made for their introduction.

The purpose of these teams is to allow members to step into a proactive role that is sustainable for everyone. For example, one team member might enjoy expressing their artistic skills in making cards with messages that counter the "voices" of the trauma team and arrange to send one three times a week to the person who convened the nurturing team. Once the work of these teams is under way, the person who has convened the nurturing team often experiences fewer crises.

Other Forms of Traumatic Experience

So far, this chapter has focused on domestic abuse, peer abuse, and sexual assault. These are particularly common forms of traumatic experience in many contexts. The ideas conveyed here, however, are also relevant in situations of public violence. As part of my work, I visit places of significant devastation and meet with survivors of torture and trauma from Rwanda, Iraq, and elsewhere. Wherever there is profound hardship, there are also people taking steps to care for their loved ones, to hold on to dreams, and to create a better future for the next generation.[9]

To offer a glimpse of children's responses to trauma in broader contexts of harm, the following document was put together from the words of children from a Palestinian family that lives in the Gaza Strip. These children had fled from their neighborhood during an extended military operation in which their homes were surrounded by tanks, fired on, occupied, or demolished. They managed to escape after twelve days to stay with relatives in what they thought would be a safer place. In this new neighborhood, however, a further military incursion occurred, meaning that the children were again subjected to tanks, helicopters, missiles, and gunfire. A narrative therapist, Sue Mitchell, was asked to meet with these children. In the course of her conversations with them, she wrote down the children's tips for other families who have to face a military attack:

How to Manage the Effects of a Military Attack

Tips for Children from the Children of the Aidini Family[10]

During the Attack
- It's important to support each other, to catch each other. Look at each other's faces; if you see that someone is distressed, talk to him or her.
- Keep your mind on the future; imagine the day when you'll be safe again.
- If you have no food, remember Ramadan. It is possible to go for long periods without any food or drink.
- Practice patience.

After the Attack
- Make sure you have times to be together and laugh.
- Talk together.
- Invent games that make you laugh and help you breathe.

- Keep studying–this is a good way to fight.
- Practice patience; patience is the key to well-being.
- Care for each other. Invite kids who are suffering to play with you.
- Eat olives; the olive tree is the tree of peace.

Just as Paul, earlier in this chapter, found it significant to make a contribution to other children experiencing peer abuse, the children of the Aidini family were enthusiastic about sharing their knowledge with other children facing military attack. Once we begin to acknowledge people's responses to trauma and what it is that they give value to, we can start sharing our survival skills and making contributions to one another.

Changing the Broader Culture

There is a wider challenge here. Every time we turn on our televisions, open our newspapers, or click on an online news report, we are likely to read descriptions of trauma, disaster, and injustice. We are much less likely to read of how children, young people, and adults are taking steps to protect themselves and others from the abuses they are being subjected to. We are much less likely to learn of the skills they are using to give comfort, provide care, or seek safety.

How can we change the broader culture so that we continue to broadcast and be outraged and saddened by acts of cruelty, violence, and dispossession; and yet at the same time begin to equally broadcast and honor tender and inspiring survival stories, as well as people's acts of care and protection? We can each play a part in this by honoring the survival skills of others–and by honoring our own.

Notes

1. Michael White had profound reservations about therapists encouraging people to revisit, relive, or re-experience memories of trauma. He believed this could inadvertently retraumatize people. In the following quotation, he describes the hazards involved when therapists invite people to relive traumatic memory (referring to this as revisiting the "site" of trauma):

First things first. There is no excuse for people to experience re-traumatisation within the context of therapy. Distress yes, re-traumatisation no. I believe that the notion of healing practices based on the imperative of returning to the site of the abuse in order to re-experience this is a highly questionable notion, and, as well, dangerous . . . To simply encourage people to return to the site of trauma can . . . contribute to renewed trauma and it can incite renewed actions of self-abuse . . . At the time that these people were subject to abuse, they had no power, they had no choice–they were trapped. In response to such impossible and agonising circumstances, many developed rather fantastic mechanisms that enabled them to escape the abusive context–not materially, but to spirit themselves away in mind. Others used what little manoeuvering space that was available to them to create experiences of self-sustenance–and, in circumstances such as these, this is simply an extraordinary achievement. Now let me pose a question. In requiring people to return to the site of trauma, are we not reproducing conditions that are entrapping, that are dispossessing people of choice? And there are other questions that we could ask about this. In requiring people to return to the site of trauma, are we not also unwittingly reproducing our culture's phobia about flight? Are we not being just too complicit with this culture's imperative of "facing up"? And in this complicity, are we not closing down the possibilities that might be available to people for the honoring of the special skills and the personal qualities that made it possible for them to navigate through the dark hours of their lives and into the present? (White, 1995a, p. 85)

2. Angel Yuen can be contacted via www.narrativetherapycentre .com.

3. For more information about the experiences of men who have experienced childhood sexual abuse, see O'Leary, 1998.

4. The quotations from members of Silent Too Long were first published in *Silent Too Long,* 2000, p. 66.

5. These examples were first published in a project initiated by Shona Russell and David Denborough. See Dulwich Centre, 2008a.

6. This example was also taken from Dulwich Centre, 2008a.

7. The exercise in relation to self-parenting was originally published in White, 1988.

8. The ideas about nurturing teams come from White, 1995a.

9. For further reading about the use of narrative ideas in broader contexts of trauma and hardship, see Abu-Rayyan, 2009; Denborough, 2010, 2012a; and Denborough, Freedman, and White, 2008. For further reading about people's responses in contexts of trauma, see Wade, 1997; White, 2004b, 2005.

10. This document was first published in Mitchell, 2005.

CHAPTER 8

Saying Hello Again
When We Have Lost
Someone We Love

THE CONCEPT OF "saying hello again" to a lost loved one can transform the experience of grief. It can also assist us to see how we are carrying on the legacies of those we have loved. This chapter invites you to experience a different way of relating to grief and loss. It offers you the chance to "say hello again" to the person who has passed away and to see yourself, once again, through their loving eyes. To introduce this idea, let's meet Mary and then John, two people who spoke with Michael White in therapy. Here is what Michael says about Mary:[1]

Mary was forty-three years old when she sought help for what she described as "unresolved loss." Some six years earlier, her husband, Ron, had died suddenly from heart failure. This was entirely unexpected. Until that time, everything had been fine for Mary. She and Ron had enjoyed a "rich and loving" friendship, one that they both valued very highly.

Upon Ron's death, Mary's world fell apart. Grief-stricken and feeling "numbed," she "simply went through the motions of life," not experiencing consolation from any quarter. Her numbness survived a number of attempts to "work through" her grief via counselling. Medication had not provided relief. Despite this, Mary persisted in her attempts to achieve some sense of well-being by consulting therapists and "working on acceptance" over the next five years.

At my first meeting with Mary, she said that she had all but given up hope that she would ever regain even a semblance of well-being. She thought she would never be able to say good-bye. After Mary put me in touch with her despair, I invited her to escape the "deadly serious" consequences of Ron's death.

I wondered aloud whether saying good-bye was a helpful idea anyway, and about whether it might be a better idea to say hello to Ron. Further, I told Mary that the desolation she so keenly experienced might mean that she had said good-bye just too well. Mary's response was one of puzzlement and surprise. Had she heard what she thought she had? I repeated my thoughts and saw, for the first time, a spark in her.

I then asked if she would be interested in experimenting with saying hello to Ron, or if she thought he was buried too deep for her to entertain this idea. Mary began to sob; it was easy sobbing, not desperate. I waited. After ten or fifteen minutes, she suddenly said, "Yes, he's been buried too deep for me." She smiled and then said that it might be helpful to "dig him up a bit." So I began to ask some questions:

- If you were seeing yourself through Ron's eyes right now, what would you be noticing about yourself that you could appreciate?
- What difference would it make to how you feel if you were appreciating this in yourself right now?

- What do you know about yourself that you are awakened to when you bring alive the enjoyable things that Ron knew about you?
- What difference would it make to you if you kept this realization about yourself alive on a day-to-day basis?
- What difference would feeling this way make in the steps that you could take to get back into life?
- How could you let others know that you have reclaimed some of the discoveries about yourself that were clearly visible to Ron, and that you personally find attractive?
- How would being aware of that which has not been visible to you for the past six years enable you to intervene in your life?
- What difference will knowing what you now know about yourself make in the next step you take?
- In taking this next step, what else do you think you might find out about yourself that could be important for you to know?

Mary struggled with these questions through alternating bursts of sadness and joy. Over the two subsequent sessions, she shared with me the important rediscoveries that she was making about herself and life. At follow-up some twelve months later, Mary said, "It's strange, but when I discovered that Ron didn't have to die for me, that I didn't have to separate from him, I became less preoccupied with him and life was richer."

When John came to therapy with Michael, the problem he initially came to speak about was not grief at all.[2]

John was thirty-nine years old when he consulted me about long-standing "difficulties with self-esteem." He couldn't recall not having a critical attitude toward himself. Throughout his life he had hungered for approval and recognition from others. For this, he hated himself all the more, believing that he lacked substance as a person and that this was clearly apparent to others.

John considered himself loved by his wife and children and believed that his experience of parenting had gone some way toward countering his nagging self-doubt—but it never went far enough. His self-doubt was so easily triggered by what he considered to be the most trivial of circumstances. On various occasions he had sought professional advice, but he had not experienced the relief that he was seeking.

In view of the long history of John's self-rejection, I asked for further details about his life. He told me that, as far as he knew, he had had a happy childhood until the death of his mother at the tender age of seven, just before his eighth birthday. No one in the family had coped with this at all well and, for a time, John's father had been a lost person to everyone, including himself. John had vivid recall of the events surrounding his mother's death. He had experienced disbelief for a considerable time, always expecting that she would show up around the next corner. He then became entirely heartbroken. Eventually his father remarried to a caring person, "but things were never really the same again."

I asked John what difference it would have made in how he felt about himself now if his mother hadn't died. At this point, he began to get tearful. I asked him, didn't he think she might have gone missing from his life for too long? Was it really helpful for her to remain absent from his life? He looked surprised. Would he mind if I asked more questions? "No, that would be fine." I proceeded with the following:

• What did your mother see when she looked at you through her loving eyes?

- How did she know these things about you?
- What can you now see in yourself that had been lost to you for many years?
- What difference would it make in your relationships with others if you carried this knowledge with you in your daily life?
- How would this make it easier for you to be your own person rather than a person who exists for others?
- What could you do to introduce others to this new picture of yourself as a person?
- How would bringing others into this new picture of your person enable you to nurture yourself more?
- In what way would such an experience of nurturing yourself affect your relationship with yourself?

I met with John on three further occasions at two-week intervals, and then for a follow-up eight months later. Over this time, he took various steps to keep his mother's "picture" of him in circulation, and arrived at a new relationship with himself, one that was self-accepting rather than self-rejecting. He no longer felt vulnerable to those events that had previously driven him into self-doubt.

Mary's and John's stories are two examples of "saying hello again" conversations. Is there someone who was dear to you but is no longer alive? Have you taken steps to say good-bye to this person, as we are encouraged to do in Western culture? Would you be interested in saying hello to them again?

I am referring here to people who were good to us while they were alive. If we have lost people we love who were good to us some of the time but abusive to us at other times, then saying hello again is more complex, and we will address this later in the chapter. For now, if there is someone in your own life who is dear to you and who has passed on, consider these questions and write your responses below:

• What did _____ see when they looked at you through their loving eyes?

• How did they know these things about you?

• If they could be with you today, what would they say to you about the efforts you are making in your life? What words of encouragement would they offer?

• What difference would it make to your relationships with others if you carried this knowledge with you in your daily life?

About Saying Hello Again

The idea of "saying hello again" to someone who has passed away may sound strange. In recent times, within Western culture, the dominant metaphor of grieving has involved only "saying good-bye." We are often invited to undertake a step-by-step process of saying good-bye, moving on, and accepting a reality that no longer includes the lost loved one. In his work as a therapist, however, Michael White discovered that some people struggle profoundly with trying to say good-bye to those who have died, and that, in these circumstances, saying hello again can be highly significant. This idea is supported by the work of anthropologist Barbara Myerhoff (1982):

> Freud . . . suggests that the completion of the mourning process requires that those left behind develop a new reality which no longer includes what has been lost. But . . . it must be added that full recovery from mourning may restore what has been lost, maintaining it through incorporation into the present. Full recollection and retention may be as vital to recovery and wellbeing as forfeiting memories. (p. 111)

Of course, when someone we love dies, there is much to say good-bye to, including a material reality, hopes and expectations, and so on. So perhaps what we are really discussing here is a process of "saying good-bye and then saying hello again."

We Are Not Alone

One of the effects of grief and loss can be a sense of profound loneliness and isolation. As well as saying hello again to those we have lost, sometimes it can make a difference to share and exchange different ways that people have responded to losses. Perhaps what you have learned about grief could assist someone else who is going through difficult times now.

Because of past and current injustices, Aboriginal and Torres Strait Islander communities in Australia face unbearable losses of loved ones. In recent years, these communities have begun to share some of their special skills in responding to these losses. Stories, documents, and songs are being shared across the nation to offer company, solace, solidarity, and valuable ideas about how to get through times of profound sorrow.

One of the most influential documents came from the Port Augusta Aboriginal community. Carolynanha Johnson played a key part in its development[3] and has given her permission for this extract to be shared here:

Responding to So Many Losses

Special Skills of the Port Augusta Aboriginal Community

Recently, there have been so many losses in our families and in our community. Some of these deaths have been particularly difficult as they have been deaths of young people, and death through suicide or violence. We have experienced so many losses, one after the other. It has been a real struggle to get through. There has been too much sadness. This document has been created from a discussion we had together in Port Augusta to talk about our grief, what is important to us, and the ways in which we have been responding to so many losses.

Asking Questions
When some deaths seem particularly unfair, when it seems so very wrong, it can make it harder to continue with life.

When the person who has died should still be with us, this can leave us not knowing where to look, not knowing where to go or who to turn to. At times like this, all we have left are questions: Why did this happen? What is going wrong if our young people are having such a hard time? How can we support other young people? What steps can be put in place to ensure this doesn't happen to others? These are important questions. They show respect for the person who has died. They show respect for all young people. They show respect for life.

Dreams

Some of us have dreams in which our loved ones visit us. Even though they have passed away, they come to us in our dreams. We dream of walking together again across the land. These images sustain us; they convince us that we will walk together again one day. Sometimes we also have a sense that our lost loved one is communicating with us—telling us that everything is all right. On the anniversary of people's deaths, sometimes our loved one comes back to us in our dreams to tell us they are going now and not to worry about them. This can lift a weight from our shoulders. We know they are now okay. Sometimes our dreams have a different sort of message. One of us even dreamt that a lost loved one saw us at the pokies [poker machines at a casino]. He gave one of us a slap and then left! That seems a pretty clear message! Mostly, though, our loved ones offer us comfort through dreams. Even though they are no longer with us here on earth, they are still offering us comfort. Sometimes we also feel a touch on our shoulders and know it is our mother's touch. Or we feel her rubbing our back as she always did when we were children. Feeling the kindness of loved ones in our dreams or through their touch helps us to continue with our lives.

Spirituality

For some of us, spiritual beliefs and practices are what help us to get through. Faith that one day we will meet again with those who have passed away sustains us. Acts of prayer are also significant. Knowing that someone is listening and will answer our prayers can make a difference.

Crying Together

When one of us is feeling low, others feel it too. We have skills in feeling each other's pain and suffering. In this way we share grief. I remember one time, I was sitting in front of a photograph of my mother and crying when my relatives walked in. They sat down beside me, put their arms around me, and started to cry too. "What are we crying about?" they said. I told them, and we sat in sadness together.

Tears and Laughter

For us, tears and laughter go together. As well as sharing sorrow together, we also re-tell the funny stories from a person's life. It's important we don't forget these funny stories. We talk about the good times, we laugh; this makes us feel sad, and then we laugh again. Sometimes looking at a particular photograph might bring tears, another time a burst of laughter! For us, tears and laughter go together. There are many very funny stories. For instance, when we asked one of our young ones if he could remember his grandfather's voice and what he used to say, this young one said, "Yes, sure, I remember him. I remember him saying, 'Can you shut up, you bastard!'" It was very funny! Another time, we were coming back from a funeral on a bus and there was a lot of laughter as we hurried along. As the bus was going a little too fast, one young guy yelled out, "I don't think Grandpa wants to see us again quite so soon; we only just said good-bye to him!" There are many ways in which we grieve with tears and laughter.

They Are With Us Forever

Because we love them so much, we may grieve forever for those who have died. But we will never forget them. They might not be here with us, but we have them in our hearts and in our minds.

Exchanging Stories and Knowledge

These stories from Port Augusta were shared not only with other Aboriginal communities in Australia but also in the United States. Messages have been sent back and forth, including the following words from Julie Moss of the Keetoowah Band of the Cherokee:

My name is Julie Moss. I am an Indigenous woman of North America. I am a Keetoowah Cherokee. We came originally from the Southeast of the USA but were forcibly removed just a few short generations ago and marched to Oklahoma Indian Territory, which is where we are now. We still follow and practice traditional ways. I am the wife of one of the leaders of our ceremonies. We have this message for you.

We send greetings and good tidings to you from here in Indian country, Oklahoma. I send greetings on behalf of the Keetoowah Band of the Cherokee.

Our hearts go out to your community, including your elders and ancestors. Thank you for sharing with us your visions *and dreams. We honor these. In your words we have sensed a strength in traditions and ceremonies and a beautiful view of life.*

We stand in solidarity with you and hold you in our prayers. We are also using our traditions and our dreams and visions as a firebreak in tough times.

We are reading and telling your stories all the way over here in Indian country. Your stories are a teaching, just like our dreams are a teaching. Your stories about remaining connected to those who have passed away are a teaching for other peoples. This is something to be honored, acknowledged, and treated as sacred.

When we have a sudden or violent death or a suicide here, it leaves a lot of pain and questions behind. It's like someone has been snatched from life and our people are still reaching out to that person. Many times, in order to achieve peace for ourselves and our community, we hold a sweat lodge ceremony. Our sweat house is considered sacred and holy. We fast before we enter, and inside we sing tribal songs and offer prayers. It is our holy place, and this is where our healing happens. Peace is achieved in the doorway between this world and the next. The person who has gone comes to that doorway, and then after the ceremony they move on, and we are allowed to go on with our lives.

The next time that we hold our ceremony we will remember you all in our prayers. We will pray for you inside our sweat lodge. We will speak of how you sent your stories to us and what this has meant to us. We will request prayers for you in our lodge.

Thank you for your teachings and your beautiful way of looking at life.

Sending Messages and Sharing Forms of Remembrance

Have you also experienced too many losses? As you read the words and stories from Port Augusta, do any of their themes resonate for you? If so, perhaps you or others you know would be interested in sending a message back to this community. The Port Augusta Aboriginal community continues to face profound losses, and they are interested in sharing their knowledge with others, no matter where you may be reading their words.

The process of sharing knowledge about ways of responding to grief can play a part in reducing the sense of loneliness in loss. What you have learned through your losses may be able to make a contribution to somebody who is grieving now.

If you would like to send a response to the people of Port Augusta,[4] here are some questions to use as a guide:

- When you read the document from Port Augusta, which of their words or stories were significant to you? Was there a particular part that stood out? Does this connect with something that is important to you in your own life?
- Have their words made you think about anything differently, or remember what is important to you? What contribution have their words made to you?
- What are some of your special skills in dealing with losses? Can you share a story of one special skill that you use in your life, or one way that you offer solace or comfort to others in times of loss? In your culture, are there particular ways of grieving that are significant to you?

When Grief Is Raw

You may be reading these words because you have recently lost a loved one. In recognition of this, I wish to share with you the story of Almas Jeninie, a colleague who lives in Ramallah, Palestine. One day, I received an email from Almas telling me that her husband, Daim, had died unexpectedly and that she was struggling terribly as a consequence. I was on the other side of the world, but it seemed important to create a context in which Almas could speak about her loss, her love, her lament. So I sent to her a series of questions and asked her to write responses to whichever ones she chose. I told her that I would share her written responses with other women who were also experiencing grief.

Here are the questions that I sent to Almas:[5]

Physical places associated with comfort

- Are there particular places that you go to that bring comfort in relation to loss?
- Why are these places special? Can you tell a story about these places?
- What do you do at these places?

Memories

- Are there particular memories that you deliberately revisit and that bring you comfort?
- If so, could you share a story about some of these?
- Are there other memories that you know it's better not to think about? How do you keep these memories at bay?

Your own history

- Have there been other times, earlier in your life, when you have had to deal with loss or grief?
- If so, how did you go about this? Please tell us a story about this.

- What were the hardest parts then?
- Were there others who supported you through this time? If so, what did they do? And what would they do if they were with you now?

Missing and lamenting

- What are some of the things that you miss the most in relation to the person who has died?
- Why are these the things that matter most at this time? Why are these things important to you?
- Have they always been important to you? How did they come to be so significant?
- Who else would know that these are some of the things that matter most to you in life?

The spiritual

- As you are dealing with issues of grief and loss, are you also engaged in spiritual matters in some way?
- If so, what are the sorts of "spiritual conversations" you are having at the moment—with God, with yourself, with others?
- What do you think these spiritual conversations say about what is important to you?
- Has this always been important to you in life? Who did you learn these spiritual values from?

Culture

- Are there particular ways of responding to grief and loss within your culture that are significant to you?
- Why are these significant? How do you participate in these?
- Are there aspects of your culture's ways of responding to grief and loss that do not fit so well for you?
- If so, how do you find ways to grieve in your own ways?

Different realms of expression

- At this time of loss, are there particular smells, sounds, songs, textures, tastes, dances, and so forth that are particularly important to you?
- If so, can you explain why these are especially important to you now?
- Are there rituals that you are finding helpful? These might be rituals that celebrate the person's life, or rituals of memory, or any other sorts of rituals.

Life looking different

- Is there anything about life that looks different because of your loss?
- Are there things you are noticing differently or doing differently?
- Are there ways in which you want to live the rest of your life differently?

Legacy

- Are there any things about the person who has died that you want to "carry on" in your life?
- Are there particular values, dreams, or ways of being that you wish to continue?
- Are there ways in which you are already doing this? If so, can you share a story about this?
- What things do you think the person would want you to continue in your life?
- What stories about them do you think they would want to see passed on in your family?
- Whom might they choose to be the keeper and teller of these stories?

Others

- Are there ways in which you are trying to support others in coming to terms with this loss? How? Can you tell us a story about this?
- Where did you learn these ways of trying to take care of others at times like this?
- What is the history of these skills?
- Who would be least surprised to know that you have these skills, even when you yourself are struggling?
- Are there ways in which others (your friends, children, colleagues) are trying to support you? If so, have there been certain actions that have meant a lot to you? Can you tell a story about this?
- Why were these actions significant to you?
- Were you able to receive their care? How?

Contributions to each other's lives

- When you think about the person who has died, what difference did they make to your life?
- What has that contribution made possible that would otherwise not have been possible?
- How do you think that person would feel if they knew this?
- What did you bring to their life that made a difference to them?

If the person who has died could be there with you now

- If the person who has died could be there with you now, what do you think they would say about how you are trying to deal with their dying?
- What would they notice about your grief and loss? What would they think of your special ways of dealing with this?

- What would they say to you at this time? And how would they say it?

Over a number of weeks, Almas considered these questions and wrote responses to me. With her agreement, I will share some of these responses here:[6]

Physical Places Associated with Comfort

Over the last few months, my room (our room; Daim's and mine) has somehow turned into a shrine. It wasn't anything I planned to do. I found a really great picture of him pulling at a cigarette with his eyes all scrunched up—a very "Marlboro/ cowboy/rugged man" type of picture—and blew it up. I hung it right over my side of the bed. The sides of the bureau mirror are all stuffed with pictures. A wedding picture of ours hangs— has always hung—on another wall. My screensaver is a picture of Daim up in a tangerine tree with dew all over him, and he's looking great with a devilish smile and sparkly eyes. His side of the bed still has his glasses, pack of cigarettes, and cell phone on the nightstand. His robe hangs, as it always has, behind the door. He was a university professor, so his pile of books and papers still lies right by the computer. When he first died, I refused to go into the room for over a month. Having others bring me out clothes got impractical, so I eventually braved the space, but until about a month ago I slept on the couch.

Then one day, Mom came over and sat on the edge of the bed while I worked on the computer. After she left, I began smoothing out the covers, and his smell rose up. I tore back the covers, buried my face in his pillow and slept—my first real sleep in months. So, I moved back in. I sincerely doubt that the pillows and sheets still smell like him, but somehow, he's there. I did a 180-degree turn—instead of sleeping on the couch and avoiding the entire room, I began looking forward to being there. I don't know if turning the room into a shrine—and the fact that time, in some ways, stopped in that room—is very "healthy," but I did, and it has. My brother-in-law is uncomfortable with Daim's eyes smiling down from every wall, as well as his clothes and books, but right now, it's a comfort to me.

Memories That Are Deliberately Revisited and Those You Try to Keep at Bay

I have so many good memories. I remember calling him at work the very day he died and telling him, "Hey, there's a picture of me on our work website!" He asked for the address and opened it up while we were on the phone. He printed it out and showed it to all his colleagues. He brought it home with him that day and sat and read the text. When I asked him why he was so absorbed in the article, he said, "Because you're in it. I'm interested in everything you do." That memory always makes me smile!

I remember once my youngest son, Sharif, asked Daim, "Why do you and Mom fight sometimes?" Without missing a beat, he threw Sharif over his shoulder and said, "So that we can make up!"

So many times he'd actually hide my makeup bag, and when I'd begin the search for it he'd always say, "I really don't think there's room for improvement."

During the month of Ramadan, he would wake the kids up before dawn and prepare an elaborate breakfast for them. I never could fathom the idea of waking up at 3 a.m., eating a huge meal, and going back to sleep, so he took over. Right before daybreak, he'd bring a glass of water to me, gently wake me up, and say, "Just please drink this."

I could probably go on forever about memories that I deliberately revisit; I have sixteen years of memories that bring me comfort. Sometimes I spend too much time there and worry that I'm not dealing with reality. The other day I was off in la-la land and my daughter walked by and touched my face. She said, "You look so pretty with that smile on your face; what're you thinking about?"

There are other memories that I don't want to think about that relate to the days before he died. Four days before he died we sat around talking and just being until about midnight and then headed off to bed. I managed to beat him in and watched him take off his clothes so that he could get his pajamas on. Suddenly, he turned his back to me and put both hands on the bureau. He motioned for me to be quiet. I practically stopped breathing and listened. I was expecting a military incursion, shooting, something like that. After about thirty seconds, I whispered that I couldn't hear anything. He turned around, and I was out of bed in less than a second. He was lemon yellow and his undershirt, fresh less than sixty seconds before, was literally soaked. He looked like someone had poured a bucket of water on him. His hair, wet with sweat, began to curl. In short, he looked like he'd taken a shower with his clothes on. But his color. It was a color I had never seen before, and my father died from cancer—so that's saying a lot.

I got him to the hospital, but after many hours and various tests, the doctors released him and said he was fine. Why didn't I scream, "How stupid are you?" I didn't. I insisted that he be admitted and went home. Two hours later he had been discharged. By 8 a.m. the next morning, we were back at the hospital, but again the doctors said there was nothing wrong—perhaps a gas attack from eating an okra dish, or a speck of sand in his urinary tract. A third doctor we consulted said that he should stay away from air-conditioning.

Two days later, Daim died as a result of a massive heart attack when driving his car. There were way too many signs. I knew he was sick. I could have screamed louder, insisted harder. Forced him to a hospital in Israel or Jordan. He died from massive heart failure in less than thirty seconds. He was forty-four.

I don't like to go back to those four days because it hurts so very, very badly. But Guilt is really powerful and demands attention. It will never let me forget. Guilt can sometimes make the memory of those four days override the memories I've made over sixteen years. But Guilt understands that I have three children to care for, and tries to visit only at night when the kids are sleeping and everything's quiet.

Your Own History of Dealing With Loss and Grief

There is a story about the history of grief and loss that I must tell. It is about my father and me. Now that I've lost my husband, this story about my father is even more meaningful. My father actually died twice. I spent the last forty-eight hours of his life sitting behind him holding him at an angle that was comfortable for him. He couldn't lie down because he felt he was suffocating, and he couldn't sit up on his own—he kept sliding down. So, I sat behind him, on the bed, and kept him comfortable. People kept coming to say good-bye, and when they'd see him and cry, I'd hate them. They were destroying his spirit.

The doctor came in to check him at 4 p.m. and carried him out of my arms and set him on a chair. I used the time to straighten the bed; the doctor was fumbling in his bag. When we looked up, Dad had stopped breathing. Everyone had been so impressed with my strength and practicality, but I went crazy then. I ran over and began to shake him and scream, "No, yaba, not now, not yet; I have to tell you—I still didn't tell you. Please, yaba, please, the boys will be here soon; don't do this, not now, please not now . . ." The doctor literally poured a bottle of water over his head and punched him in the chest. He woke up and was clearly disoriented. I'll never forget what he said, and others heard him say it too: "But I was home. I want to go back home; please let me go back home." I got really close to his face and began gently wiping the water off. I said, "Yaba, you are home. The boys will be here in a couple of hours. Please wait for the boys."

He did. As soon as the boys came in, they rushed upstairs. Dad looked at them and recognized them. They cried softly and kneeled before him while I was still holding him. I motioned for them not to cry, but they couldn't help it. They had seen him less than two months ago and couldn't believe how quickly he had deteriorated. He kissed their heads and said, "Why are you crying? I should be crying for you. I get to go home while you're still here. It's so beautiful. I get to go home; don't cry for me." Of course, by then, everyone was bawling. But the conviction in his face was amazing: There was absolutely no fear or reluctance; he actually seemed eager. He turned his head back as much as possible and said to me, "I want to sleep now. Please lay me down; I want to go back home." So, I did. We took turns monitoring his breathing until 11:30 p.m., when he passed away.

Sometimes my father visits me in my dreams. The first time, I actually sleepwalked. About a week after my father died, I heard a knock at the front door. When I got to the front door, there was a really powerful bright light as well as a string of lights at the front door. A group of similar lights were in the back. The light at the front was my dad—I heard his voice, but I knew it was him before he spoke. I asked him what he was doing outside the front door—to come in, it was cold and windy. He said, "We come here every morning to check on you, but yaba, if you keep this up, I won't come anymore." He was referring to my crying, shock, and withdrawal—I knew exactly what he meant. I said, "Yeah, okay, fine, but come in; it's so cold." He said that he couldn't; he was "all over" and couldn't stay too long in any one place. He said he wouldn't wake me up anymore, but he knew I'd remember this visit (and I always have, like it was yesterday), and that I should know that he was always around.

It was actually very cold, and my crazy-with-fear husband found me at about 5:30 a.m. on the front porch, which is glassed in, sitting on the couch in a long T-shirt. There were leaves everywhere and the front door was open.

He still visits in my dreams occasionally, and I say it: I tell him that I love him, that I understand, that I forgive him for being so distant. I thank him for taking so much care of me. I thank him for instilling pride in my culture in me. I tell him I respect him for being so brave, for leaving his country to secure a future for his children without ever forgetting who he *was. But that's just in my dreams; I don't know if he can hear me. I do know though that I will never, ever forget the peaceful smile on his face when he stopped breathing.*

The Spiritual

My spirituality is currently on a roller-coaster ride. My religion was instilled in me, pretty much by force, as a child—so it never really had any true meaning. I tried to keep it up right after I got married, but Daim wasn't really religious at the time either, so we had weak attempts. The "break down and fall on your knees believing to the marrow of your bone in God" happened to us both at the same time, when our first child, Mimi, was born. I know a lot of people explain life scientifically, but I truly believe that God had everything to do with that perfect creation. I was astounded. I treated her like a miracle, and not at all because we had trouble having her. I truly believe that giving life is a miracle. I again believed in God when I lost my father; he was so comfortable about passing away.

After Daim's death, though, my beliefs have become like a roller coaster. Daim didn't want to die. When I took him to the hospital a couple of days before he died, he actually said that the angel of death had come for him and he turned him away saying that his wife and children still needed him. We talked about going to the kids' graduations and weddings. We talked about being grandparents. We joked about who would take care of whom. We had plans and dreams; he had plans and dreams. I wonder why God didn't take me instead of Daim. I wonder why God thinks I can bear this pain; I wonder how I will. People try to console me by reciting infor-

mation on predestination. I can't swallow that yet. Daim died from medical negligence—God had nothing to do with it. God can't possibly be so cruel.

I believe that Daim is now in a better place. I believe he is at peace and comfortable. That is reassuring in many ways, but then I think, "But he was at peace here, he was comfortable here, he wanted to be here." If I have to look for things to be grateful for, I am grateful that he didn't suffer. We traced his phone calls and movements, and he died in less than a minute; when I saw him, he looked like he was sleeping.

I think my loss has shaken my spirit and my faith. It's inside of me though, like a bunch of butterflies in a closed jar. If you shake the jar, they'll flutter around for a while, even panic. But eventually, they'll all settle down again. It shook me hard, really hard, to think that God is cruel. I just hope that the butterflies settle down before the moral of the story flashes by and I miss it in a whirl of wings.

Particular Smells, Sounds, Songs, Textures, Tastes, Dances That Are Important . . .
I really like these questions. Sometimes something will remind me, and people around me will have no idea, and I'll smile—or pull away to control my tears. I've started smoking. Not really. I'm not addicted or anything; sometimes I'll light one up and just let it burn down in the ashtray. Not a lovely or romantic smell I must admit, but it reminds me of him. He also has a pack of cherry vanilla cigars by his bedstand. I won't dare burn them; then they'd be gone. But sometimes I just open up the tin and smell them. I remember how his hands and clothes would smell. I'd complain, of course, but now it reminds me.

As for sounds, Daim set me up for a nightmare right before he left! Sharif's our little monkey; very sly, sweet, and smooth. Daim had taken him to music school during the summer, about a month before he died. Sharif tried out all the instruments and kept going back to the cello. About two hours later, they came home with a cello and promises of music lessons to begin within a month. I was really confused—why the cello? Not very Eastern, not very Arabic, not what we expected! So now, six months later, I get to deal with the whine and squeal of the cello as Sharif "practices." I get to tell him how wonderfully he's progressing. I look up at the sky and mumble, "Thanks, Daim! Hope you can hear this!" I imagine he can; it is loud and horrible enough to wake the dead!

Cultural Ways of Grieving: Those That Fit and Those That Do Not

I spent much of my childhood in the United States, so I have lived in two cultures. Here in Palestine, we have some interesting cultural responses to loss. Some are beautiful, some infuriate me, and some I will never forgive.

The Islamic culture has a very practical view on death. We believe that, from the moment you are born, it is predetermined when exactly you will die. There is absolutely nothing you can do about it. You may have some effect on how you die—for example, by not smoking you may prevent death by lung cancer—but you're still going to die on that day. I don't think this is actually in the Koran, so this may be more cultural than religious, but a lot of speculation is also given on how one dies. For example, my dad was such a generous, respected figure that when he died from lung cancer two months after diagnosis, and only really suffered for about five days, no one was surprised. Dying from cancer can be very drawn out and painful, but Dad didn't really suffer extensively, supposedly because he was "a good man." I don't really buy into this idea, because a lot of incredible people suffer immensely while dying, but our culture believes that a torturous death is God's way of speeding up the punishment you are sure to receive in the afterworld. A lot of people here also talk about "punishment in the grave"—horror stories about how the grave caves in on you and angels torture you as you await judgment day. These are horrific ideas to me and I try to stay away from them.

Anyway, when a person dies, it is supposedly predestined, and therefore excessive grief is frowned on. Some people actually say that wailing and lamentation will cause the dead pain, as if you're protesting God's will. This a very final, very practical way of looking at death, but it doesn't necessarily create room for expressions of pain, hurt, and sudden love loss.

Another religious custom involves the immediate burial of the dead. We have a saying, "Respect for the dead is in the burial." The body is bathed, wrapped in a sheet, prayed over, and put in the ground. Ideally, it should be in the ground by the next call to prayer, or within twenty-four hours maximum. Usually the burial takes place at the noon prayers—these are the biggest prayers, where the largest amount of people join in, so it's the most honoring.

Throughout the entire condolence period (three days), men and women are kept very, very separated. There are very different rituals for men and women. For instance, once Daim had been bathed for burial, I was not allowed to touch him. Those women whom he can't marry—like his mother, daughter, and niece—can hug, kiss, and touch all they want, but as his wife, I would "dirty" him. I would make him "unclean." I really can't comment on how I feel about that little bit of culture right now. It's still way too much for me to comprehend.

During the three-day funeral reception, recordings of the Koran being recited are supposed to be played nonstop and bitter coffee is served. Daim's mom refused to do either. She refused to believe that this was a funeral. She refused to believe that her son was dead. I felt so much pain for her but was caught in a crossroads. My daughter, Mimi, wanted the Koran. She told me it would help her dad get into heaven. I wanted the Koran because I felt that if the Koran was being recited, well-wishers would be quiet. I was amazed that people came, each for ten minutes maximum, and were actually swapping recipes and talking about their children, cooking, and cleaning. Even at times of death, life goes on.

I spent a whole lot of time in the bedroom with Mimi. People kept coming in to tell me that people wanted to offer me condolences, that I should be outside, that I was being rude. That's when I pulled my "bicultural" card: I didn't understand; I meant no harm.

After the three-day reception in Jenin, we went back to Ramallah. We had another three-day reception there. Believe it or not, we had to rent a hall in the municipality! Police were called in to close roads. Still, when I think about the thousands of people who came, I well up with tears. This is an aspect of our culture that still surprises me. The president sent a telegram. Everyone from Birzeit University, including staff from all departments and students, came every day. Representative groups from the Palestinian Authority, everyone (parents, teachers) from my kids' schools, everyone from my workplace, and swarms of people I didn't even know. We hired someone to serve the bitter coffee, and he told us that he was going through over 2,000 plastic coffee cups a day. Bear in mind that we only accepted guests from 5 p.m. to 10 p.m. There were people outside, inside, everywhere. The newspaper was plastered with condolences for over a week (the normal time is three days). We were all grieving, but I can't deny that I felt somehow proud.

Less than ten days later, I had to start dealing with legal things. Of course, if I had seen a mental health doctor, I would definitely have been diagnosed as being "in shock," among other things. I was going to Sharia court and signing things. I wanted to give all of my inheritance to my children, but stopped at the last moment. I decided that I would inherit, and while I was alive, divide it equally among my three children in the form of gifts. I don't like the Islamic rule that girls inherit one-half of what boys inherit. So, somehow, I had the sense of mind to straighten that out.

Another cultural ritual is "cleaning up." We are supposed to give away the possessions of the deceased to those who are needy. I decided not to participate in this. At least, not yet. So many people have encouraged me to give away Daim's things; poor people would benefit greatly. Well, sorry to be selfish, but I'm not there yet. How can I give away sweaters that smell like him? How can I give away his shorts with splotches of paint all over them, that he wore around the house, that were missing the top button (we'd joke that his growing belly helped keep the shorts in place and that a button would only restrict the growth!)?

Right now, culture is encouraging me to move on. Get out of black, put some makeup on, cut my hair. I don't wear black on purpose, and I do wear colors, but as my friend noticed,

I no longer dress to impress, I dress to cover my body, and my hand is attracted to dark colors. I can't even imagine looking at myself in the mirror and caring long enough to put makeup on, and don't think I will ever, ever cut my hair. Daim used to spend hours running his hands through it and smelling it. When I would lie on his lap at night, he would smooth it over his thigh. I don't think I can ever cut it. Of course, the culture doesn't care if I cut it; everyone just wants me to cover my hair, to wear the headscarf, but Daim was really against that too, so I don't think I'll be doing that either!

As I wrote at the very beginning of this piece, Daim is everywhere in my house. I won't dispose of him, or give him away. I grieve for him every minute, for what he's missed. Nothing will ever fill up the trench that he's left behind, but he was so proud of me, and I can't let him down. Some days, when I'm too tired to open my eyes, I push myself for him. He's a part of me, so even though I grieve, I believe he's still there. He's in his children, in me, in his house, his car; he's everywhere.

Life looking different

To be honest, everything about life looks different now. So much has lost meaning; other things have so much meaning that I can't touch or look at them. For the time being, I've given up on changing the world. Worse, sometimes I'm noticing an ugly bitterness that comes to visit. Sick people who come out fine, for example. My first thought is, how come they get a miracle and I didn't? At times it can feel like I have an internal battle of good versus evil going on. I consciously shake my head and remind myself of the sixteen years I spent with Daim. Our three beautiful children are beyond the definition of miracle.

And I have found a strength. I'm going to try and see where that takes me. Right after Daim's death, my brother-in-law sat down with me and tried to explain property and financial issues. I just kept shaking my head and telling him I didn't care, I was fine with any decisions he made; I asked him to take care of everything. He held my hand, looked me straight in the eye, and said, very firmly, "I'm sorry, but you no longer have that luxury. You have to understand everything so you can take care of everything." I didn't get it at the time, but now, every time I just want to give up, I can hear him saying, "You no longer have that luxury." Daim was my luxury. There are husbands, and then there are soul mates and best friends who happen to be your husband. I lost so much more than my husband, but I think I'm starting to see Strength. Our house is literally falling apart right now, and sometimes I spend the whole day filling up cracks and sweeping up debris, but somewhere along the line I found Strength. I'm not too sure I want to deal with Strength right now, because she's really weak and needs a lot of attention that I can't give her right now. I heard, though, that Strength gets strong on her own, when you're not looking. I hope that, even if I neglect her, I'll find her when I need her the most.

The Present and the Project

Almas did find and continues to find Strength. In fact, over the last few years she has worked for a groundbreaking Palestinian women's organization dedicated to supporting women's financial independence. Her writings about her grief have also supported women in different parts of the world as part of a broader project.

If you are in the midst of grief, we would like to invite you to be part of this continuing project. Please consider any of the questions that I initially sent to Almas (pp. 216–220) and write your own responses. If you know of others in your local context who are also grieving, you may choose to do this process with them and share your writings with each other.

Alternatively, you may be interested in lodging your writings with our "responding to grief" project. We will separate your name and address from your writings so that your words will be anonymous. They will then be made available to others who are grieving, just as Almas has made her words available to others.[7]

Please return to the questions that I sent to Almas and choose whichever ones appeal to you at this time. There is no need to respond to them in any particular order. Almas decided she would respond to one theme each week, but everyone's time frame is different and everyone has their own way of grieving.

Two Important Considerations

Experiences of grief are not separate from the rest of life. All the complications and complexities of daily life, including issues of gender and power, are present in how we grieve. For instance, over time, Almas came to realize that some aspects of her experience of grief were powerfully influenced by the degree to which she was dependent upon first her father and then her husband. If women's lives are socially and financially dependent on the men in their lives, then this will influence experiences of grief. It may be that some women who lose a male partner will wish to say good-bye to or rethink certain aspects of past dependence while still cherishing the person who has died. This has been true for Almas. Her decision to change jobs and work for an organization dedicated to supporting women's financial independence is not separate from her experience of grief.

It is also significant to acknowledge that people's grief is sometimes complicated by experiences of violence or other forms of abuse. If the person who has died tyrannized other people, or if there was a lot of conflict or misunderstanding, then relating to the person's death can be complex. Responses to death in these circumstances can be quite different, as death may have brought a sense of relief as well as other responses. If this has been true for you, the following questions may be relevant to consider:

- Are there things you are relieved to be no longer experiencing? Can you share a story about these? Why are you relieved to be no longer experiencing this?
- If another person was trying to work out how to relate to the memory of a loved one who had been cruel to them (or with whom they had been in conflict), would there be any story from your own life that you would be willing to share with them?
- If you had a chance to say something now to the person who has died, would you want to? If so, what would it be? Has this changed over time?
- Is there anything about the person's life or the person's death that has led you to want to live your life in a different way? Why is this important to you? Can you share a story about how you put this into practice in your life?

The Expectations of Others

Sometimes, after a death or loss, the expectations of how one "should" grieve can be confusing. Expressions of sadness are socially accepted and expected, while expressions of rage or regret may be less welcomed. It may be seen as strange if the grieving person does not express certain feelings in particular ways. At the same time, for those who have been in a hidden or illicit relationship with someone who has died, the experience of loss can be a very private one.

- Have there been ways in which your responses to death or loss have been outside the expectations of others?
- How have you been able to craft your own ways of responding? How do these ways reflect what is important to you?
- Can you share a story about some of your unique forms of response?

Transition

Times of grief and loss are often times of transition.

- Are there certain parts of life that you have moved away from as a result of this transition? Are there things you are no longer interested in doing, being a part of, or participating in? If so, what are they?
- Are there aspects of life that you have become more engaged in or moved toward as a result of this transition? If so, can you share a story about what this means to you?

The following story was sent to us by Judy, who hopes that her experience of complicated grief will be of assistance to others[8].

When the relationship has been fraught with conflict or violence, this creates another dimension to the grief process. In my own situation, there was a feeling of relief—relief that I no longer had to live with fear. In the previous few months, I had been stalked and had had threats made on my life. Fear was something that I had lived with for many years, and it has traveled with me through most of my life. Then, after the initial shock and feeling of relief, I found fear in my life again and it was hard to let it go. I thought that there was nothing stopping him from getting to me now that he was dead. I thought he was haunting my family home. So, after a while, I sold my house, and that was helpful in allowing me to feel safe again.

The greatest challenge has been dealing with guilt. He had told me many times if I didn't take him back he would either kill me or himself. I felt responsible for his death. I thought, "If I had taken him back he would still be alive." Guilt was a major restraint to my moving on. For a long time I believed that I could have done more, been a better wife. Now I think, "Yes, I could have done things differently, but I did the best I knew how at the time."

Because of the circumstances of his death, people would avoid me. I have since heard they didn't know what to say. I interpreted that behavior as blaming me for his death. I had many irrational ideas. My experience, however, has shown me the way to a better life. I have moved from desperation, and then hope, to a life of achievement. I still have my struggles, but I move through them much more quickly. I have accomplished more than I ever believed I would both personally and professionally; this has only happened because of my experience. I am now in the privileged position of hearing the stories of others and assisting them in seeing other ways of being—of helping them move forward in their lives to a place that they want to be.

My experience has given me the understanding to support other women dealing with situations like mine. On a personal note, I have four beautiful adult children, two boys and two girls, all in healthy, respectful, long-term relationships, and

seven beautiful granddaughters. Some people say that chil-
dren repeat the patterns of their parents. This may be true in
some cases, but many choose healthy, happy lifestyles. I believe
my direction in life has added to their lives and made them
more compassionate, stronger, and self-assured, too.

If you have experienced complicated grief, perhaps you would like to consider writing a response to the questions listed above. If so, we would welcome your contribution to the grief project. It seems vitally important that people find company and acknowledgment in complex experiences of grief.

Looking Back, Looking Forward

This chapter has offered a number of different ways of "saying hello again" to those we have lost, as well as ways of sharing special skills and knowledge about grief.[9] How we think about death and those who have died makes a real difference in how we think about our lives. It also makes a difference in how we think about our own mortality, which is the theme of the next chapter.

Notes

1. Mary's story was first published in the groundbreaking paper "Saying Hullo Again: The Incorporation of the Lost Relationship in the Resolution of Grief" (White, 1988).
2. John's story was also first published in White, 1988.
3. Aunty Barbara Wingard, Djapirri Mununggirritj, and Cheryl White have also played key roles in this process. To read more about the ways in which Aboriginal Australian communities are exchanging knowledge and stories about ways of responding to

    grief, see http://www.dulwichcentre.com.au/linking-stories-and-initiatives.pdf

4. You can email a message to us at dulwich@dulwichcentre .com.au, and we will then send it back to Port Augusta via Carolynanha Johnson.

5. I drafted these questions, and several colleagues contributed to them: Margie Pitcher from Australia, Gitta Leibeherr from Switzerland, and Lorraine Hedtke from the United States.

6. Almas's writings first appeared in Dulwich Centre, 2008b.

7. You can send writings via email (dulwich@dulwichcentre.com .au) or post (Dulwich Centre, Hutt St., P.O. Box 7192, Adelaide 5000, South Australia). If you do choose to send your writings, we will send you an acknowledgment that we have received them.

8. Judy's story first appeared in Dulwich Centre, 2008b.

9. To read more about narrative approaches to grief, see Hedtke and Winslade, 2004.

CHAPTER 9

Legacy and Memory: When We Are Facing Our Final Chapter

THIS CHAPTER FOCUSES on considerations of legacy and memory. How can considering the legacies that we will leave behind help us to face our own mortality? How can "spiritual wills" assist us when we are facing our "final chapter" here on earth? And how can letters to loved ones provide comfort if we are concerned that as we age we may no longer be able to remember who we are?

Death and Dying: Living on in the Lives of Others

When we are facing death, either because we are growing old or because of illness or injury,* it is a time to consider what will be carried on from our lives. While our bodies are sure to die, our spirits are sure to live on in the memories, lives, and conversations of others. In many cultures, this is honored and clearly recognized:

> [In some cultures a] distinction is drawn around the death of the body and the survival of the personhood of the deceased

---

* Please note that this chapter has not been written for people who are affected by suicidal thoughts. If you are considering suicide or are affected by suicidal thoughts, I'd suggest you speak about this with someone, be it a friend, community leader, and/or professional.

... At a particular point in time after the ritualized goodbye to the dead body, the relatives of the bereaved assemble again, this time to take on the virtues of the deceased, or if you like, the spirit of the deceased. Perhaps we could say that the spirit of the deceased is regained. (David Epston in White & Epston, 1991, pp. 28–29)

And so, as we are approaching death, we can ask ourselves, "What piece of my life will survive physical death?" What legacies will we be leaving behind on earth? These legacies may not be grand, and they may be hard to think of at first, particularly if our lives have been lived outside the mainstream.

When two of Cheryl White's dear friends were dying of AIDS in the early 1990s, she asked David Epston and Michael White to collaborate to come up with ways of working with those who are dying, particularly those who have been marginalized by the dominant culture, like gay men. In their collaborations, they discovered that it made a difference if the dying person was thought of as a benefactor who could invite certain people to be the beneficiaries of their legacies. If we include certain virtues or values that we have carried in our lives as part of the legacy that we wish to leave, it can broaden our view of life and death.

There may be more than one legacy that we wish to leave. Ted, for instance, was determined to leave behind a beautiful garden that he had created. He was also determined "never to be a bother to anyone ever again." Ted was HIV positive and took part in a narrative gathering in the 1990s in Adelaide. When we inquired about the histories of these two legacies that he wished to leave, we were told a story about "Aunty Nature."[1]

Aunty Nature

Spirituality of the Garden
by Ted

When I was diagnosed with HIV, I joined the euthanasia society and distributed leaflets to doctors, to family, and to friends. I prepaid and planned my own funeral. Throughout my life people have always told me that I was a bother to them. I am determined that I will never be a bother to anyone ever again—especially in death.

I do not have trust in human beings. This was removed long ago. I was sold by my family when I was only three years old. When, many years later, I came to Australia, I was a foreigner, then a gay foreigner, and then an HIV-positive gay foreigner. I have learned that at the end of the day you are by yourself; you're on your own.

But to be honest, I do not believe this completely, because I am with my garden, the trees, the flowers and butterflies. This is my spirituality, to spend time with nature. Some people call nature Mother Nature, but I call her Aunty Nature. When trust is gone, you can turn to her and to the trees—they do not hit you; they offer only comfort, not violence. To spend time in my garden brings me great joy and peacefulness. There is a serenity there and simple beauty.

When you ask me why I call her Aunty Nature, well, there is a story I can tell about that. It begins when I was small child shortly after WW2. We were very poor at home, in the mountains of what used to be Yugoslavia—it is now Slovenia, an independent country. There were ten of us children, and there was very little food.

I don't have any idea where it came from, but I vaguely remember my Aunty having a hessian [burlap] bag. She would throw this hessian [burlap] bag over her shoulder and would set off walking from village to village. She was a professional beggar. When she would come back home, she would always empty the bag upside down, and things would fall out. Bread, fruit, and I do remember that once there was a salami or sausage. I thought, gosh, aunties are wonderful. And so if there is anything wonderful, I always think of my aunty with her bag of surprises. Nature also has many surprises, and that is why I call her Aunty Nature.

What I learned from my aunt became very important later. As I mentioned before, I was sold at the age of three to go and work on a farm. Anyone who was old enough to hold a tool of some kind was given away or sold or adopted. When I couldn't cope anymore at the farm to which I had been sold, I ran away. I had, over the years, become used to hiding in the forest for many days at a time. Trees had been a comfort for me then, a place to run away to. But this time I had decided that I would not go back to the farm. There are many other horrible stories about what happened on this farm, and I am very lucky to be alive. So this time I hid in the forest for three months. I thought to myself, if my aunty could beg (she wasn't alive anymore), then why couldn't I? And so I took up my aunty's profession.

I went from house to house, from village to village, begging for food. That was how I survived. Of course, before too long the weather became very cold. Living under the tree wasn't much fun in autumn when the rain and snow started to come, so I had to go back to the farm. Fortunately, though, that was when the social security came and took me away. They placed

me in an orphanage—and that was wonderful. I enjoyed my
time in the orphanage. This was in the early 1960s. In that
part of the world people were still very poor in those days.
Being up in the mountains with goats, civilization was very
different there than what we know here today.

I have plans for what I am going to do when I am ninety,
but I have life and my death organized, prepared for. I will
never be a bother to anyone ever again. And I will continue
to delight in the butterflies, the trees in my garden.

Think for a moment about what virtues or values you
would like to leave others. In considering this, it then becomes
possible to create a special sort of document—a secondary will
of our legacies, learnings, and virtues. While wills usually
have to do with physical property, these secondary wills relate
to what could be called "spiritual property."[2] Here is an example, as told by narrative therapist David Epston:

> I was working with a woman who was terminally ill. Shortly
> before her death she made me the agent of her will and testa-
> ment. As part of my duties as agent, it was my responsibility
> to distribute, to appropriate persons, copies of a very important
> document. This document included a testimony to the sexual
> abuse that she experienced as a young person, some thoughts
> about how others might free themselves from the long-term
> effects of such abuse, and a message of hope. (David Epston
> in White & Epston, 1991, p. 31)

Creating a Secondary Will

If you know someone who is facing their own death
because of old age or illness, perhaps you can assist them in

creating a secondary will in relation to learnings or values that they would like to pass on to others. Alternatively, you might consider the legacies that you wish to leave to others, as well as how you are trying to carry on the legacies that have been bequeathed to you. These may be small, such as a love of gardening, or an interest in sports, or a sense of humor, or an appreciation of beauty, or courage.

Here is an example of a secondary will. Jacinta[3] had been diagnosed with cancer, and while she was optimistic that she might be able to overcome this, she decided it was an important time to consider her life and legacies.

Will and Testament of Legacy, Learnings, and Virtues

I, Jacinta, residing at 1500 Campbell Avenue, New Orleans, being of sound mind, hereby declare this to be my Will and Testament of legacy, learning, and virtues.

1. I acknowledge that the following virtues and values were passed down to me (either from people I met in the course of my life, or from people I did not meet personally but heard about, read about, or listened to, and who were significant to me):

- *Love of nature* from *my grandmother who loved the morning bird song*
- *Reading to learn* from *my fifth-grade teacher, Mrs. Simons, who believed in me when no one else did*
- *Kindness* from *Dusty, my cat, who cuddles with me when I need her*

2. I acknowledge that I have learned the following things during the course of this lifetime, including learnings that have come from difficult times:

- *Determination* from *the time I left home at 15 and traveled interstate to Grandma's place*
- *That you have to laugh* from *the time when it was just me and my friend Rose, and we'd gotten ourselves lost and just had to wait till morning light. We laughed our way through the night because we knew we wouldn't sleep.*

3. I propose that the following virtues, values, and learnings that were passed down to me be distributed to the following people and pets, who I think could make most use of them:

- *Reading to learn*   to *my niece Georgina*
- *Love of nature*   to *our neighborhood environmental group, the Waterwatchers*
- *Kindness*   to *strangers*

These are some of the ways I have already tried to share these virtues and values that were passed on to me, and the learnings that I have accumulated over time:

- *I read to Georgina, and we make up stories together.*
- *Each week I meet with the Waterwatchers, and together we are trying to clean the waterways.*
- *The kindness that Dusty has shown to me, I try to show to strangers—people I meet in the supermarket or when walking.*

4. I direct that the following characteristics *not* be passed on to any of my dear ones, and that they end with me:

- *The shakes and sorrows that I sometimes feel*
- *The voice of abuse that makes me doubt myself*

I would like others to understand that I don't want these passed on because . . .

No one deserves to be abused.

5. I wish to pass on this message of hope:

Georgina, you are only four, so it may be a while before you can read this. Perhaps I will ask your mom to read you these words from Aunt Jacinta. I want you to know what you have brought to my life and to the life of your mom. I have loved our story times together. You are a great listener, and stories and characters seem to come alive when we are together. Your imagination helps mine. I also really appreciate how kind you are to Dusty. Dusty has been very important to me in my life, and I know that if anything was to happen to me you would take good care of her. Thank you for being such a kind person, Georgie.

Dated this 15th day of May 2013

I will update this Will and Testament of legacy, learnings, and virtues every three months.

Signed by: Jacinta

Witnessed by: Dusty

If you would like to create your own secondary will or assist someone else in doing so, you may like to use Jacinta's template:

Will and Testament of Legacy, Learnings, and Virtues

I, _____, residing at _____, being of sound mind, hereby declare this to be my Will and Testament of legacy, learning, and virtues.

1. I acknowledge that the following virtues and values were passed down to me (either from people I met in the course of my life, or from people I did not meet personally but heard about, read about, or listened to, and who were significant to me):*

- _____ from _____

- _____ from _____

- _____ from _____

- _____ from _____

- _____ from _____

2. I acknowledge that I have learned the following things during the course of this lifetime, including learnings that came from difficult times:

- _____ from the time when _____

- _____ from the time when _____

- _____ from the time when _____

3. I propose that the following virtues, values, and learnings that were passed down to me be distributed to the following people and pets, who I think could make most use of them:

- _____ to _____

- _____ to _____

- _____ to _____

---

*This list can also include virtues inherited from people who have passed away, pets, and invisible friends.

These are some of the ways I have already tried to share these virtues and values that were passed on to me, and the learnings that I have accumulated over time:

• _____

• _____

• _____

4. I direct that the following characteristics *not* be passed on to any of my dear ones and that they end with me:

• _____

• _____

• _____

I would like others to understand that I don't want these passed on because . . .

_____

5. I wish to pass on a message of hope to someone I have noticed making a contribution to the lives of others, or to those who have been through experiences similar to my own. This is the message I wish to convey:

_____

_____

_____

_____

_____

Dated this _____ day of _____ 20___

I will next update this Will and Testament of legacy, learnings, and virtues on the _____ day of _____ 20___

_____
Signed by:

_____
Witnessed by:

Name:

Address:

Shared Memory

It is not only when we are facing death that we may think about legacy, but also if we are faced with the loss of memory. Recently I had the pleasure to work alongside people with early-onset dementia and their family members. This was in relation to a theater production that I was writing in collaboration with my sister, who is a dancer and director.[4] My role was to meet with people with early-onset dementia and their family members, gather together their words and stories, and craft these stories into a theater production that would do justice to their lives and experiences.

Prior to my involvement in this show, the word *dementia* evoked only a sense of lurking dread. My grandmother experienced dementia, and my memories of this are depressing—it's as if the times I visited her in the nursing home are cast without color. My first community forum with people with early-onset dementia and those who love them somehow opened a window and brought new light. Together we heard of so many ways in which these couples and families are protecting what is important to them. While we heard stories of loss, sorrow, and frustration, we also laughed together and learned how people are finding ways to share memory, distribute among themselves what could otherwise be burdens, and continue to delight in love and life. This has been highly significant to me. While the word *dementia* still evokes sorrow and grief, it now also evokes stories of kindnesses and acts of grace and dignity. My experiences with people with early-onset dementia and their families have somehow changed my relationship to memory and even to my own history.

To convey this, it's necessary for me to introduce you to the world and words of people with early-onset dementia and those who love them:

> Imagine this. It is becoming increasingly difficult to discern the difference between the present and the past, between what is familiar and what is foreign. Events that took place just minutes ago are being constantly erased, while memories that you have been able to keep at bay for decades now come rushing toward you. Despite the explorations of poets, novelists, doctors, scientists, and philosophers, the realm of memory remains a great mystery. If a loved one starts to lose their memories, what role can we play in holding onto them? And if our parent is no longer the person we know, how can we care for them in the present and also honor their memory?

The following stories convey both the effects of dementia and the ways in which people with dementia and those who care about them respond to these situations:[5]

Loss
The person with dementia has to let go of the things that they used to do. And this means so many different sorts of losses. My mom was a professional portrait artist. Watching her art-

istry change and deteriorate was a source of profound sad-
ness to me. I could feel what was going on inside her mind.

The Last Two Years Were the Best Two Years

My father was brought up in a rigid household during the
depression and world war. In some ways, the last two years
of his life were the best two years of my relationship with him.
Somehow the Alzheimer's released the rigidity of his childhood,
and this was a gift to me. He told me that he loved me for the
first time. He told me that he trusted me. And this was so dif-
ferent to the memories that I had of my childhood years, of the
leather strap on my backside. What's more, in his last years,
touch became so much more significant between us. Tactile
communication became all important. Sometimes he became
too tactile! But still, there were times of kind physical contact
that meant a lot to me. It was as though these years balanced the
memories of my life. During this time it was like I was weighing
up different memories. I couldn't have asked for anything better.

A Shift in the Balance of the Relationship

In my childhood, my mother looked after me in every way.
Now things have turned around completely. I was born
dependent on her, and she will die dependent on me. There is
a symmetry about this, a poetry almost. It is not always easy,
but it makes a difference to remember this balance.

Fantasy

Sometimes fantasy worlds develop and can bring great joy. He
used to tell us with great excitement stories about the times he
was the captain of the rowing team and the football team. But
he never had been—these were stories from his father's life! He

also used to tell us about managing Elvis and Frank Sinatra. They were great stories, elaborate fantasies!

• • •

That reminds me of how my father kept telling us about the conversations he would have in the mornings with the man in the room next to him. He'd tell us all about these chats and how much he enjoyed them. And then one day, we realized that the person in the room next to him could not speak! Only then did we realize that my father was actually referring to conversations he was having with his own image in the mirror when he was shaving!

The Longest Farewell
On first hearing the diagnosis, a common reaction is to realize that you will lose a friend (in my case a wife of forty-nine years). So at first I did panic a bit to tap her memory for stories of her childhood, to take overseas trips to say good-bye to relatives and friends, etc. But then the situation seemed to change only slowly. So it's like a farewell, but one that stretches on and on and on—the longest farewell of all.

Longer-Term Memories
Alzheimer's is not about losing all memories. While short-term memories may disappear, longer-term memories can become all the more vivid. I remember when my mother suddenly started to tell me things that I had never known. She told me that when she was pregnant with me, her doctor had suggested that she have an abortion. My mother was forty-six at the time, my father was seventy, and the doctor was concerned about

complications for my mother and for the baby. My mother told me, however, "I wasn't going to do that with you." It was a profound conversation, like a jewel. Somehow, due to the disease, I learned a little more about aspects of my own history.

That was true for my father also. The older memories become even stronger, indelible. My father had served during the war in PNG and he had never told us about this. One day, we were sitting in the garden in the nursing home, and the bushes were moving with a breeze in a way that seemed to stir up a memory. He asked, "Has the battalion been fed?" and then, "Have you got the pistol and rifle?"

Dad started to lose his words though. And as he lost his words he replaced them with numbers. He was a Chartered Accountant and he used to say, "18, 19, 20." One day in the nursing home, I was sitting beside Dad. As he appeared to be sleeping, one of the nurses asked me, "What sort of work did your father do?" When I said, "He was an accountant," my dad didn't even open up his eyes; he just said, "Chartered Accountant." That still makes me smile.

Later, at the Christmas party in the same nursing home, they had a man playing the guitar, and when he sang "It's a Long Way to Tipperary," my dad joined in. At this stage, I hadn't heard Dad speak for months, so when he sang, I had to leave the room. I went into another room and cried. When speaking is gone, it seems that singing sometimes takes its place.

• • •

When this was mentioned in the group, one person with younger-onset Alzheimer's said, "God, I hope not!" And the room erupted in laughter.

Memory Loss

When the person you love no longer remembers what you have said, it has a lot of implications. On the positive side, you can crack the same joke time and again and get a laugh! But on the other hand, if there is a death of someone they love, then they relive this loss time and again, and this can be devastating.

Traveling through Time

My father thought I was his wife. He thought he was forty and tried to propose to me. We did a book of his life so that I could try to use it to explain who I was. Even so, he would say, "Yes, yes, yes, but I've still got to ask you to marry me."

• • •

I would touch my mother's hand and hold it and she would say, "Oh I like that. Except that you're a girl, you could be Jack." And this was the opening to hear stories of her earlier life and the man she had loved but never married. Whenever I held her hand she always went back to Jack. They were very moving conversations. And she would find solace in telling me that she "would never have made a good farmer's wife."

• • •

In one aged care facility I worked, the staff would say, "Ask Harold what year it is." And he would always answer 1942. And so we would travel with him back to 1942. We would go with the flow. It is the only way to be with somebody if they are living the past.

It Affects Everyone

When someone in a family is affected by Alzheimer's, it's like the family has the diagnosis, not just the individual. Some-

times a family can collapse overnight; the relationships can break down and this can be very difficult. Sometimes daughters are pressured by their brothers to care for parents. Sometimes gay men having been rejected by their family years earlier are suddenly expected to come back and care for their parent because they do not have their own children. Alzheimer's affects everyone. And if it is your parent who receives the diagnosis, then you've also got the thought in the back of your mind, "Will my own memory be affected one day?"

What seems really important is that care for people with Alzheimer's is shared, not left to any one person. Sometimes family members leave it all to one person in the family (often a woman), and this makes things very difficult. But sometimes a carer might also choose to become the central and "special" carer in a person's life and then they get burnt out, and this is also a hazard. It seems important that care is shared.

Conversation

Conversation can be difficult when Alzheimer's is around. I had to realize that the conversation I was having with my mother was not the same conversation she was having with me. I remember she used to say to me, "Jesus, you're a shocking conversationalist." Eventually, when things were stuck in the conversation and my mother was frustrated with my response, I learned to say, "I don't know. What do you want me to say?" She would then tell me what to say, I would give that answer, and we could continue!

Keeping What We Could the Same

Right to the very end, there were some things that he could still enjoy. He had been a great sportsman, and he would continue to watch golf and football on television. We had always loved to dance. And right up to the time when he could no longer walk, we would dance together: put the jazz on and dance in the kitchen. Looking back, I feel that we all did the very best that we could. He kept his dignity. Despite everything that changed, we found a way for him to remain the person he always was.

A Wonderful Old Fur Coat

I remember a particular woman who I used to work with [in a care facility for the elderly]. She had been there for five years, and by the time I arrived she never spoke. I had to immediately move into her reality, which was entirely nonverbal. I learned that she used to be a dancer and a patron of the arts. When she became confined to her chair, she remained highly tactile. We would use massage to soothe her and to help her to sleep. She would also love listening to music. And there was a wonderful old fur coat that we would wrap around her. It was like we were wrapping her past around her. As soon as she was encircled in it, she would become calm. I've always remembered that wonderful old coat.

Shared Humor

In the early stages, shared humor can make all the difference. And remembering the stories years later seems significant too. My mother used to insist that I was her sister, not her daughter. When I would try to insist that she was my mother, she would say, "Jeez, one of us looks good for our age." It was very funny.

Two-Way Caring

It's important to realize that especially in the early times, there is a two-way caring. I remember one day tears had come. It had been a really hard time and he couldn't talk about it, but he simply put his arms around me. He knew I was upset, and while there weren't words, there was loving touch. It made a huge difference to me.

• • •

During the early times, there are so many difficult preparations to be made, like wills and arrangements. And some of this is so difficult to do. It is so painful to face. But my husband went through all of this, and I knew these were acts of great care for me. There was one day in particular where we had had to go through awful practical preparations. At the end of this, we had endured too much and he said, "Let's go and have tea at the Windsor." We went there and it was totally booked out, but the look on our faces must have told a story and they quickly set us up a special table. This was an important ritual for us. There are many different examples of this sort of two-way caring.

Children
Sometimes children will respond to the person with dementia in different ways than us adults. For instance, I remember we told our son that "Gran forgets things," so when he next saw her, he said, "Grandma, what do you forget?" There's something about how kids go straight to the point that is very refreshing. Also, our children will remember their grandparent in different ways than we will. They will remember the games they played together, the fun they had with each other. These are important memories to keep alive.

Living for the Moment
The changes in short-term memory create unexpected dilemmas. For example, we recently gave my wife a terrific seventieth

birthday party; the house was full of relatives and friends, balloons, numerous humorous speeches (she even made a speech herself). But the next morning she could not remember a thing about the party. It had been a huge effort on the part of her family. So you start to wonder if it was all worth it. But then you realize that a person with dementia lives only for the moment, almost literally. You can't stop giving someone a full life just because they will not remember it.

A Book of Memories

If a loved one is losing the memory of who they used to be, sometimes it's up to us to hold their memory for them. My mother made a book for Dad containing stories, photographs, and mementos from his life. This also helped the nurses and staff who looked after him. Dad used to go through the book with them, and while he couldn't always answer their questions, he liked to look at the pictures. This book contained photos from his childhood, of his teachers, of where they had holidays, pictures from his school days, and from when he was overseas where he met my mother. It also included their wedding invitation and photos and then the story of us as a family. It was very comforting for both us his family and for Dad to look through this book and retell all the stories. We also made a few large photo boards of Dad and his family for when he was in the nursing home. It was important to us that the staff in the nursing home could see what a loving and loved man he was and the sort of life he lived before he got Alzheimer's.

In It Together

A number of us regularly meet together. We are couples in which one partner has Alzheimer's. It makes it so much easier to have others to talk with who understand what is going on. We found that the carers really needed help. They felt that they were carrying the weight on their own and as if they were the only ones suffering. They didn't realize that others were doing the same thing and that the experience could be shared. And we (people with Alzheimer's) realized things too—including that it's important for us to be nice to the people who are looking after us! We've learned that it's good to do things together— to go for a meal or to a hotel or down at the beach. We also stay in touch on the phone. We call every now and again. We've learned a lot. Next week the carers are going to get together just on their own, so they will whine a bit and then get things back together! We also sometimes attend Memory Lane Café, which is run by Alzheimer's Australia. It's hard to convey just how important this has been to us. This group that we are a part of represents perhaps the most important thing that we have ever done in our lives. We're not the only ones.

A Letter to Our Dear Ones

I find these stories profoundly moving, particularly regarding the care that these people are taking in relation to preparations for the future. They have thought so much about the loss, the sharing, and the transmission of memory. What can we all learn from their hard-won knowledge? How can we apply this to our own lives? One way might be to write a letter to those who are dear to us—now, while we can still remember what's important to us.

From the words and stories shared above, the theater production *Sundowner* was created.[6] The main character is a woman with early-onset dementia, who throughout the show crafts a letter to leave to her children (one of whom is pregnant with the next generation). Here is the letter that she writes:

> *My Dear Ones,*
>
> *It's the strangest thing, no longer being able to tell what is the past and what is the present. It seems that events that took place only minutes ago are now being erased, while memories I have been able to hold at bay for decades suddenly come rushing towards me.*
>
> *No doubt it is only going to get worse. At times, now, I am no longer able to tell what is familiar and what is foreign. And that is why I am writing to you today.*
>
> *When it comes to pass that I can no longer hold the memory of who I used to be, will you hold it for me?*
>
> *I don't want this to be a burden, but if you could remember me perhaps just once a day in the evening light . . . that was always my favorite time. Hold my memory in the evening light, my dear ones.*
>
> *I don't mean any old, dusty memory of me. I don't mean a time when I was crabby or tired—let others remember those times, or better yet, let them slide into oblivion. No, I'd like you to remember something particular, something luminous.*
>
> *I guess you should have some say in it, but if I get to choose, how about you remember that day we spent at Rosebud?*
>
> *It was hot that day. Our feet had to dance across the sand to avoid being scorched. And we plunged into the sea together. The others were laughing at us—with us, I recall.*

We'd all been through so much that summer, and somehow we'd found our way through together. Yes, remember me then, if you would.

I wish I could promise to always remember you, but that's a promise I can no longer make.

I have loved you the very best that I could for all the years that have been.

Your devoted mother

P.S. There is just one more thing, while I remember! When you are with child, treasure the memories you make together. That child of yours will live with those memories for a lifetime.

A narrative therapist in Hong Kong is now supporting people with early-onset dementia in writing such a letter to *their* "dear ones." In these letters, the writers acknowledge what their loved ones have contributed to them, reveal any regrets they may have about how they have treated their loved ones, and highlight particular memories they hope others will carry into the future.

Perhaps there will come a day when we can no longer recall who we are. Writing such a letter to "our dear ones" now might make all the difference down the road.

Exercise One: Write a Letter to Your Dear Ones

Take a pen and paper (just for old time's sake), or open a new document on your tablet or laptop, and begin to craft a letter to a loved one. This loved one may be older or younger than you. They may be someone you see regularly or not at all these days. They may be a friend, a colleague, a sibling or another family member, an invisible friend, or a pet. Within this letter you could include:

- Specific ways in which this loved one has made a contribution to your life
- Any regrets that you may have about how you have treated this loved one
- Two particularly good memories that you shared with this loved one. Try to describe these in vivid detail, evoking all the different senses associated with each memory. What did it look like that day? What did it smell like, feel like, taste like?
- An explanation of what these memories mean to you
- An invitation to your loved one to hold these memories and honor them for you both

Exercise Two: Recording the Memories of Others

Alternatively, you might like to take the advice of a caretaker of someone with early-onset dementia:

> I would really suggest that you take notes of things that your loved ones say. Note down the family stories, even the ones you think you will never forget, in fact, especially the ones you think you will never forget.[7]

Is there someone whose life you appreciate? If so, perhaps you can make time next week to sit with them and write down (with their permission) some of your favorite stories about them. It doesn't matter what age this person is; they might be younger than you. All that matters is that there are stories associated with them that you would like not to be forgotten.

Perhaps you can also ask this person about some of their favorite memories:

- Ask them questions so that they can describe these memories in vivid detail, evoking all the different senses associated with each memory. What did it look like that day? What did it smell like, feel like, taste like?
- Ask them to describe what these memories mean to them.

As you converse with your loved one, you might like to let them know what these memories and stories mean to you. Find some way of conveying that you will hold, honor, and care for these memories and stories.

Looking Back, Looking Forward

This chapter has focused on considerations of legacy and memory. I have invited you to think about the legacies of values, virtues, and learning that you would like to leave to others. To do so, and to create a secondary or "spiritual" will, can sometimes alter not only how we face our deaths, but also how we live our lives.

Considerations of memory can also be significant. The day will come when it will be up to others to hold our memories for us. We can prepare for this day and I hope the ideas in this chapter of writing letters to loved ones and recording the memories of others can assist in this.

Recognizing the legacies and memories that we will leave behind us places our lives in a broader context. The final chapter of this book focuses on where our story fits in the bigger picture.

Notes

1. Ted's story was first published in the Dulwich Centre, 2000, and is republished here with permission.
2. David Epston discussed these ideas of "spiritual property" and alternative wills in White & Epston, 1991.
3. Jacinta is a composite character.
4. This theater production, *Sundowner*, was produced by KAGE (www.kage.com.au). Jack Sach, Jill Linklater, Shirley Rutherford, and Christine Bolt from Alzheimer's Australia (Vic) played significant roles in enabling *Sundowner* to become a reality.
5. The quotations from people with early-onset Alzheimer's and their caretakers are from the article "Special Knowledge and Stories about Dementia" (Alzheimer's Australia Vic Community Advisory Group & Denborough, 2011). The following people contributed their stories: Fiona Beale, Rachelle Better-Johnston, Liz Brady, Robyn Carmichael, Liz Fenwick, Pamela Hore, Carol Liavas, Megan Major, Kim Martin, Carmel McGrath, Rob McGrath, Kris Samuel, Dennis Tonks, Margaret Tonks, Tom Valenta, Tony Walsh, Paul Wenn, and Judith Wheaton.
6. The written resource most helpful to the creative team in developing *Sundowner* was the book *Contented Dementia* by Oliver James (Vermilion, London, 2009).
7. This quotation is from Alzheimer's Australia Vic Community Advisory Group & Denborough, 2011, p. 68.

CHAPTER 10

Where Does Our Story Fit in the Bigger Picture?

STORIES ABOUT OUR lives start before our birth, and they don't end with our death. We carry on the legacies, gifts, and burdens of those who have come before us, and those with whom we are connected will carry on our legacies long after we have gone.

So far in this book we have considered ways of rewriting the stories of our own lives and how we can assist others in telling the stories of their lives in ways that make them stronger. What about the bigger picture? How are the stories of our lives influenced by the actions of those who came before us? What difference can it make to how we understand our lives if we consider broader family and societal histories?

Early on in this book, we considered how we link certain events in our lives into storylines of our identity. These storylines influence how we think about our lives and the actions that we take. In this chapter, we will consider linking the storylines of our lives with the actions of our ancestors. This can put our own lives into a different perspective and add new meaning and understanding. It can even connect us to different priorities, hopes, and dreams.

This has been true for me. In the following pages I will share with you a letter I decided to write to one of my ancestors and describe what this has changed for me. I have also included a letter from Lisa Berndt, who lives in California, to one of her ancestors.

My letter and Lisa's letter both focus on trying to come to terms with profound injustices to which our ancestors contributed. The reason I am including these letters is that I believe those of us whose ancestors caused great harm have particular responsibilities. Depending on where you live and your own family histories, the letters you write may be very different. But no matter who we are, considering the bigger picture and bringing our ancestors with us can make a difference in how we rewrite the stories of our lives.

Trying to Find a Founding Father

The impetus for creating a "letter to ancestry" came when I was working alongside Jane Lester, an Aboriginal Australian woman whose extended family had been profoundly affected by what are called, here in Australia, the Stolen Generations.[1] Entire generations of children within Jane's family had been taken from their parents by the authorities and placed in mission homes. In fact, at one time the children of Jane's family made up an entire institution.[2] I was working with Jane to document some of the stories of her family, including how she was still searching for her grandmother, how she had made many profound reconnections, and how all these stories were linked with the history of the country.

As we worked together, Jane would quite often ask me about my family history and about my ancestry, and often I could not answer her questions. I had somehow left my ancestors behind. As I reflected on how little I knew of my own family history, and how it might be linked to events in the nation's past, I made a quiet vow to myself. I vowed that I would trace the histories of my family in the hope that in future conversations with Jane and others, the stories I discovered could in some way be linked and shared.

And so Jane's generosity of spirit started me on a journey through my family history. But of course the stories of my family are very different. My father was not forcibly removed from his family, nor were his siblings or his cousins. In fact, in many ways, the histories of my family could not be more different. My great-great-grandfather on my mother's side was Sir Samuel Griffith, who was instrumental in drafting the Australian constitution and went on to become the first chief justice of the country. He is considered one of the "founding fathers" of modern Australia.

In some ways my search to understand the life of Sir Samuel Griffith could not be more different than the search Jane Lester was undertaking. But there are some similarities. I would not be alive if it were not for Samuel Griffith. It is through conversations with Jane and other Indigenous colleagues that I have learned something of the importance of honoring our heritage and respecting those who lived lives dedicated to us—their children, grandchildren, great-grandchildren. But honoring ancestry is a complex process when your family histories are interwoven with the dispossession of other peoples.

One side of my ancestry was involved in literally dispossessing Aboriginal people of their land in northern Queensland. Another side was instrumental in crafting a constitution that legalized this dispossession. To quote Andrea Rieniets (1995), "What do you do when you find that your family tree has been replanted in someone else's yard?"

When I was working closely with Jane Lester, conversations about reconciliation between Indigenous and non-Indigenous Australia were occurring throughout the country. A march for reconciliation across the Sydney Harbour Bridge had recently featured hundreds of thousands of participants. The entire country, it seemed, was powerfully moved when, during the march, a small plane wrote the single word *Sorry* in the sky.[3] This was the context in which I was trying to respond to Jane's questions about my own ancestors.

In some ways, it seemed that the process of tracing my family history would involve speaking across time and across generations. And so I decided it would be most appropriate to write Samuel Griffith a letter[4]:

Dear Samuel,

I have struggled to find words to write to you. Your name is being spoken of more regularly these days, and when I hear it, or see a photograph of you, I am not quite sure what to feel. I am not sure whether to greet you with a smile, respect you with a nod, or turn away in confusion or sorrow. I imagine this would make little sense to you, you who lived a life with the finest of intentions and contributed so much to this country that I dearly love. But Samuel, I am struggling with big questions that wrap themselves around me at times. How can I honor you and all your contributions without dishonoring the original peoples of this land? And how can I honor the original peoples of this land without dishonoring you?

You know, I'd really like to talk this over with you if it were possible. But you have been dead for three times longer than I have lived. So I have sought out your letters and diaries; I have read your words, I have plowed through book after book that relates the stories of the times in which you lived. Why? you might ask. Put simply, I have come looking for you because this country that I love and cherish is trying to understand its past.

The last few years, Samuel, have changed the ways we see ourselves as Australian. We have witnessed a terrifying upsurge of racism as a right-wing party has established itself on the political landscape. We have learned of the ongoing effects of deaths in custody and the Stolen Generations of the Indigenous Peoples of this land. And we have seen ordinary Australians in the hundreds of thousands march for reconciliation and sign sorry books. We, non-Indigenous Australians, have searched for ways to express our profound sorrow at what has transpired in this land, and to take whatever action is necessary so that Indigenous and non-Indigenous Australia can together walk into the future.

Samuel, how can I convey what this has meant to me? As I grew up, I knew nothing of those whose spirituality pervades the land on which I learned to walk. I knew nothing of the stories and songlines that weave their way through my favorite places in the world. I didn't know this land, I didn't understand it. I lived in some way separate from it. I lived a life disconnected, separated from Australia's heartland. It wasn't until I walked into the prisons at Long Bay in Sydney that I realized that I knew so very little about Australia.

It was in the cell blocks and the inner circles of prisons that I received a second education. Some of it was pretty direct, while other aspects were tender and took time. Samuel, you were one of the early lawyers in Australia, you were the first chief justice, you played a crucial part in bringing British law and interpretation to this land. I know you did this in goodwill. I know you did this with profound skill. I know you even did this with compassion, and that for your time you were progressive. But Samuel, I have spent time in the institutions that are the foundation of that legal system. I have seen the cells where Aboriginal inmates burn oils to free the souls of those who have lived and died within them. In no way do I judge your life—I know that my own has only been possible due to yours—but I do feel great sorrow in relation to our connection to this history. The imposition of British law on Indigenous Australia has been a tragedy. Especially when Indigenous community processes offer us other ways of responding to conflicts. Throughout the world, Aboriginal communities are reclaiming the right to address their own conflicts in their own ways, and in the process they are offering us all so much. They are offering the possibility of life without prisons and the degradations they represent.

Lately, Samuel, some people have been trying to tell us that we must choose between a black armband view of Australian history, one that supposedly acknowledges only the suffering and injustice in our past, and a white blindfold view that speaks only of pride, triumph, and celebration. And yet the two do not seem so separate to me. The moments that I have felt the most intense, passionate pride in this country are those moments when collectively it seems that we are managing to address the most challenging aspects of our past. Surely coming to terms with our past in all its complexity can in itself be a source of pride.

Samuel, I was born in 1970, and for much of my life I have quietly lamented not being alive during the eras of great social change when mass social movements were altering the land-scape and imagination of nations and of the world. I lamented not being around during the anti–Vietnam War movement, the women's liberation movement, Stonewall, or, earlier still, the civil rights movement in North America.

Only last year, however, on the day of the reconciliation march across Sydney Harbour Bridge, when "Sorry" was written across the sky, did I come to understand that we are in the midst of such a time right now: a time when our history is being recon-sidered and our relationships with the past and therefore the future reimagined; a time when ordinary people are rising to the occasion to right the wrongs committed by those who have come before us and to create a different tomorrow. This moment, a hundred years since Australia became a nation, is in my view a time for celebration: a time to celebrate that we are now grap-pling with our history in all its complexity—its horrors and its wonders. A time to celebrate that there now exists a people's movement hoping to right the wrongs of this nation's past so that we can all stand together in its future.

Samuel, I am trying to understand your life, the context in which you lived. I know that so much of your life and those of your times were dedicated to the lives of us in the future. I believe this means we have profound responsibilities to those of you who have gone. I am reveling in all that you achieved, and I am seeking to play a small part in redressing that which you did not. I hope of this you would be proud. As we take more collec-tive action to redress the harmful events of this nation's past, I feel I will somehow grow more connected to my own ancestral stories. Samuel, I feel that I will continue to come to know you over future years. And one day of course, when we of the present generations are long gone, it will be up to our children, grand-children, and great-grandchildren to redress all that we have not understood.

Samuel, I do so wish you could have been here this morning to witness just a tiny sample of what life is like in this nation you played a key part in creating. But I guess in some ways you have been here. Your life has shaped every word that I have spoken this morning. I can't pretend that this process of look-ing for you is complete, that I now know how to address you or how to relate to the legacies of my family histories. I can only say that I am so glad to have come looking for you. I am so glad that I have at least written this first letter. And for this I have Indigenous Australia to thank. It seems to me that Indigenous Australia is imploring us not to forget the past, not to turn our backs on our ancestors, but instead to remember you, to reconnect with your actions, their effects and their ongoing legacies. This is, I believe, a most generous invitation, for perhaps in the process we will be coming home to our own histories. Perhaps we will find ways to relate to our ancestors' lives that do justice to the complexity and richness of this coun-try's history. I do hope so.

Yours sincerely,

Your great-great-grandson,

David

Reconnecting with my own ancestry has been highly sig-nificant to me. It has placed the stories of my life into a much longer storyline, one that started long before I was born and will continue long after my death. Reconnecting with my ancestry has also changed me. While I might have always thought that the continuing injustice toward Aboriginal people in this land was wrong, now I am personally connected to it. This is part of my story and my family's story. Since I wrote to Samuel Griffith, it feels like a duty to my own ancestry to continue to work in partnership with Aboriginal Australian friends and colleagues. But this duty and these partnerships are not a burden. They are a source of joy and connectedness. In fact, it is during moments of such partnerships that I have a sense that I am in the right place in life. Some people speak of spirituality when they talk of this. If that is the case, then finding ways to honor my ancestry by continuing to redress harm and prevent further harm is my form of spiritual practice. And when I am long gone, I hope our descendants will find ways to redress the harm we are doing now.

Family Storylines in the United States

In the United States, family storylines weave through different histories. One year after I wrote to my great-great-grandfather, the first U.S. letter to ancestry was read in Sisters Chapel at Spelman College in Atlanta, Georgia.[5] Sisters Chapel is where Martin Luther King's body was laid in state after he was assassinated. It is a place of reverence. Three speakers took part in a ritual there: Patrick Moss of the Keetoowah Band of the Cherokee; Vanessa Jackson, who spoke of African American histories and healing; and Lisa Berndt, a European American, who read out the following letter to her ancestor General Griffith Rutherford.[6]

A Letter to General Griffith Rutherford

by Lisa Berndt[7]

This morning, I would like to read to you all a letter that I have written to the great-grandfather of my great-grandfather, a man who was introduced to me as General Griffith Rutherford. But before I do, I want to tell you why this is important to me. Standing here with Native American and African American friends and colleagues is something that offers me great hope. I carry with me considerable sadness and horror about some of the actions of my ancestors. To stand with you while acknowledging all that happened in the past helps me to imagine a different future for all of us. I'd like to thank you for inviting me to be part of this event this morning and for opening the opportunity to build loving relationships with ancestors I've been reluctant to trust. Here's a beginning . . .

Dear Sir,

I am writing to you on a special occasion. This morning is an opportunity to stand together and weave histories: Native American, African American, European American. I wonder what you think of all this, being invited to this magnificent place so full of ancestors and ancestors-to-be, all with stories to tell.

To me this is important, vital, healing, this acknowledgement of what and who has come before.

It was my grandfather who first introduced me to you, General, shortly before he died. He, Grandmother, and I would sit around the kitchen table and reminisce. We'd talk about the memories we loved best, and some of the disappointments we shared. Grand-

mother would always cook a ham, and Granddad would talk about his brothers who'd passed on, his mother, and his father.

In my family and in my culture, however, there have always been patches of silence, like fog, or like ice. We all knew: You don't go in there. It felt like shame, but I'm not sure what to call it. Because of those patches of silence, it was never really clear where we came from, or what awful thing somebody had done that nobody was talking about. The ice started to crack when I learned that my grandparents had been married at a Ku Klux Klan meeting. I came to realize that what was left of Great-Granddad Lester's prestige derived from his leadership of the Klan around Paris, Texas, in the 1920s. I was horrified to discover this, and to find out more about what life was like for African Americans in North Texas at that time, but it helped make sense of things.

There are many patches of silence that I would like to traverse. So much fog to see through, so much ice I want to thaw. It is in this spirit that I am trying to know you better, General. Because your story and mine aren't separate.

I don't know much more about you than the fragments of recorded history. I know that you and your parents left Ireland for the North American colonies when you were an infant in 1721 and that your parents died on that voyage. I wonder what that was like for you. I know that cousins took you in and saw to your education in New Jersey. I know that you were trained as a surveyor, and that you worked your way through Virginia and into North Carolina, where you made your home. I know you married Mary Elizabeth, had eight children, and took part in community building and government forming. I know you were elected to the colonial legislature in North Carolina, that you voted for the Declaration of Independence, and that you loved to show your grandchildren the snuffbox George Washington gave you on a visit to your home.

These are stories that connect me to the history I learned in school, and I felt pride and belonging when my grandfather shared them with me. I also know that you joined the colonial army and that by 1776 you were a brigadier general fighting the British and Indians. I was grieved—I was horrified—to read that you led forces that burned thirty Cherokee villages: a campaign that "opened the way" for the Treaty of Long Island and the ceding of all Indian land east of the Blue Ridge. I believe you were rewarded for this action with large amounts of land.

I know that you moved in circles of power that set you up in the world of plantation finance—the economy founded on slavery—and that your lifestyle and much of your legacy were supported by the forced labor of African people. These events were documented in written history, so what I know about you are the parts you played in events that promoted the development of one nation, the United States of America, and that had disastrous effects on other nations—Indian nations and African nations. This is what I know of you. I wish I knew more.

Although I was raised in a military family, there is so much about your life and actions that I don't understand. What did you think you were doing when you set fire to those villages? What made it possible for you to do these things? Did you use words then like "collateral damage"? Did you have moments of doubt? Did the voices of the women and children stay with you? They have stayed with me.

And how did these actions shape our family's future? What are the legacies that we carry? I believe they are mixed legacies. There is no doubting the layers upon layers of privilege that we accumulated as we reaped the benefits of white supremacy and white dominance. There is no doubt that generations of our family have also taken pride when they have looked at maps of North Carolina or Tennessee and seen our family name. There is a triumphal version of our family history that glories in your achievements.

But there are also the legacies of shame. Of silence. Of the half-truths and untruths that have propped up our privilege through the years. It's very uncomfortable, queasy, disorienting, standing on stolen land, profiting from violence and stolen labor, living a fraudulent birthright. I believe it's kept us from talking to each other in life-giving ways.

General, I'd like very much to know what you think about how history remembers you. How else might you have wanted to be remembered? How did those close to you experience you? What kind of friend, neighbor, husband, and father were you? I know a little about your grandson Newt: that he struggled with alcohol and died young. I know you lost your eldest son in battle. And how did your wife, Mary Elizabeth, feel about that loss? Your absences? Your imprisonment by the British? Your campaigns? What did you tell her about what you did while you were away?

My father left for Vietnam in 1968, when I was eleven. He wrote cheerful letters about the weather and told us the tourist version when he came back. But he came back different—quieter, more angry, withdrawn. He told me much later that one of his jobs as a legal officer was to prosecute AWOL ("absent without leave") soldiers. Often he would counsel them to stay in the military. The son of an old friend heeded his counsel and was killed. This haunts him to this day. Even more haunting, he says, was the way the Vietnamese were treated in their own land. He said he could never feel at ease as an American again.

Does anything haunt you? I wonder. There is much about our past that haunts me, that fills me with sorrow. I think of those Cherokee villages; I think of the enslaved Africans on those plantations, the men and women and children terrorized by Klan violence, the villagers and boy soldiers in Vietnam, I think about the links between all these and our lives, General, and a profound sadness and remorse arises. It is a remorse that shapes many of my actions.

How can we begin to atone for those lives so exploited, ravaged, and stolen? For the ongoing effects of systems and policies that paved the way for some and blocked the way for others—that treated some as God's gift, and others as invisible or worse? Well, we know that avoiding or denying the truth doesn't work. So what if we tried it differently?

What if we took up the opportunity to learn more about, to listen deeply to, the experiences of those whose lives and livelihoods were devastated in the creation and maintenance of this nation? What if we dedicated ourselves to learning how racism was and is constructed, and to working in schools, courts, hospitals, financial institutions, governments, the arts, neighborhoods, and relationships, to take it apart? Perhaps these are legacies we can leave for my generation's great-grandchildren.

Standing here today, with African American and Native American friends and colleagues, and turning toward you, General, offers me hope. I have a longing to know and to be known by you. It is a longing that speaks to my hope that we don't have to separate from each other, that we don't have to forget where we have come from. And General, I wonder whether this might also be an important process for you. Someone asked me once, "Don't you think our ancestors keep learning too?" and I like this idea a lot. One thing I do know is that I don't have to figure this all out myself. This isn't just about you or me or my family. This is about all of us, and perhaps together we will figure out how to talk about it and where to go from here.

General, I'm not aware of traditions in my culture for contacting you, for even having this conversation. I wonder what questions you would have for me and I look forward to ongoing conversations. But I have been told that, in other people's traditions, for me to speak here today involves speaking on behalf of my ancestors. And so I'd like to close by saying, to you, with you:

It's time for you and me and all in between to come forward with the pieces of history from which we've tried so hard to protect each other and ourselves, so that we can begin to take responsibility and to participate in repairing what we can and taking a respectful place in what is to come.

Yours sincerely,

The great-granddaughter of your great-grandson,

Lisa Kathleen Rutherford Berndt

Bringing Your Ancestors with You

This book closes with one final invitation. Take a pen and paper, or open a new document, and write a letter to one of your ancestors (someone you have never met).

Perhaps, like Lisa and me, you know of an ancestor who actively participated in some form of oppression or discrimination. You may know of an ancestor who worked hard to resist such forces of oppression. Or you may choose to write to an ancestor who played a significant part in enabling you to become the person you are today.

Alternatively, letters to ancestry do not necessarily have to be written to a particular figure. Many of us don't know the details of those whose lives have come before us. I have a dear friend who was adopted from Vietnam to Australia straight after the American war in that country, and she has written beautifully about these experiences and how she has confronted the complexities of her ancestral storylines (Simmons, 2007). Other friends here in Australia know little about their ancestry. In some families it was a gift from one generation to the next *not* to pass on certain stories—to enable the next generation to have a new start, free from the burdens of history. If this is true for your family, you might like to write more generally to "your ancestors" rather than to any particular figure.

Whoever you decide to write to, here are some questions you might consider:

- What would you like to honor in relation to your ancestry? What did your ancestors' lives and actions make possible for you?
- If you have chosen to write to a particular figure, why have you chosen this person? Why are they significant to you?
- What images, thoughts, or feelings come to you when you think of this ancestor? Are there important stories, secrets, or histories that you wish to address?

- Which of the legacies and values of your ancestry are you proud of? Which do you want to continue yourself and pass on to others? Why?
- Which of these values do you not wish to continue? Why?
- Are there actions of your ancestry that, with the wisdom of hindsight, they may regret and wish to change? If so, how might you go about contributing to redress?
- If your ancestors stood against injustices, and if you are now standing against injustices, what would you like to convey to those long gone?

Once you have written your letter to your ancestor or ancestors, you may like to read it aloud as if you are reading it to the past. You may also choose to share it with friends or family to spark conversations.

Future generations

Perhaps most significant, thinking about our ancestry invites us to consider future generations and what it is that we wish to leave for them when we are gone. What steps can we take in our lifetimes to redress injustices that we were born into?[8]

I hope that considering how the storyline of your life relates to the lives of those who have come before you and those who are yet to come can provide you with a different perspective and spur you on in whatever direction you choose. This has certainly been true for me.

Notes

1. The Stolen Generations were children of Australian Aboriginal and Torres Strait Islander descent who were removed from

their families by government agencies and church missions. The removals occurred from the 1860s to the late 1960s and early 1970s.

2. The story of Jane Lester's family can be found within a beautiful book titled *Telling Our Stories in Ways That Make Us Stronger* (Wingard & Lester, 2001).

3. To read the Australian prime minister's apology to the Stolen Generations, see www.dfat.gov.au/indigenous/apology-to-stolen -generations/rudd_speech.html

4. This letter was originally published in White and Denborough, 2005b.

5. The reading of the letter to ancestry by Lisa Berndt took place at an International Narrative Therapy Conference held by Dulwich Centre at Spelman College. For more information about these conferences, see White and Denborough, 2005a, or www .dulwichcentre.com.au.

6. This letter was originally published in White and Denborough, 2005b.

7. Lisa Berndt can also be contacted via the Dulwich Centre.

8. The considerations of privilege mentioned in this chapter are associated with a wider project initiated by African American social work professor Salome Raheim. To read more about this, see http://www.dulwichcentre.com.au/privilege.html. Members of the Just Therapy Team of New Zealand (Taimalie Kiwi Tamasese, Charles Waldegrave, and Flora Tuhaka) are key contributors to this project. In the United States, Shawn Patrick is continuing the project at Texas State University. If you are interested in contributing to the project, please contact us by writing to Dulwich Centre, Hutt St., P.O. Box 7192, Adelaide 5000, South Australia, or via email at dulwich@dulwichcentre.com.au.

Looking Back, Looking Forward

THIS BOOK BEGAN with a story from my own life—a story of a thirteen-year-old boy sitting alone on a mountain ridge. In the final chapter, I included a letter to an ancestor who died close to a century ago. When I began writing, I would never have imagined that these two events would be included in these pages, but if we start exploring the storylines of our lives, unexpected connections can emerge.

I hope this is also true for you. I hope that the ideas and stories in this book have provided you with ways to take a new look at your own life, and to find a new significance in events often neglected, to find sparkling actions that are often discounted, to find fascination in experiences previously overlooked, and to find solutions to problems and predicaments in landscapes often previously considered bereft. These were the hopes that Michael White held for this book. We began this writing project together. Completing it has been a way for me to honor his memory and legacy.

I also hope that this book has provided you with ideas for ways to respond to the stories of those you care about. And I trust that the words I have shared here—words from many different people who have retold and rewritten the stories of their lives—will offer you company along the way.

For more information about narrative therapy

www.dulwichcentre.com.au
www.narrativetherapyonline.com
www.narrativeapproaches.com

References

Abu-Rayyan, N. M. (2009). Seasons of life: Ex-detainees reclaiming their lives. *International Journal of Narrative Therapy and Community Work, 2,* 24–40.

ACT Mental Health Consumers Network & Dulwich Centre. (2003). "These are not ordinary lives": The report of a mental health community gathering. *International Journal of Narrative Therapy and Community Work, 3,* 29–49.

Alzheimer's Australia Vic Community Advisory Group & Denborough, D. (2011). Special knowledge and stories about dementia. *International Journal of Narrative Therapy and Community Work, 1,* 65–71.

Brigitte, Sue, Mem, & Veronika. (1997). Power to our journeys. In C. White & D. Denborough (Eds.), *Introducing narrative therapy: A collection of practice-based writings* (pp. 203–215). Adelaide, Australia: Dulwich Centre Publications.

Bruell, A., Gatward, E., & Salesa, L. (1999). The Anti-Harassment Team: A presentation of hope. In Dulwich Centre (Ed.), *Narrative therapy and community work: A conference collection* (pp. 72–83). Adelaide, Australia: Dulwich Centre Publications.

Denborough, D. (2008). *Collective narrative practice: Responding to individuals, groups, and communities who have experienced trauma*. Adelaide, Australia: Dulwich Centre Publications.

Denborough, D. (2009). Some reflections on the legacies of Michael White. *Australian and New Zealand Journal of Family Therapy, 30*(2), 92–108.

Denborough, D. (2010). *Working with memory in the shadow of genocide: The narrative practices of Ibuka trauma counsellors*. Adelaide, Australia: Dulwich Centre Foundation International.

Denborough, D. (2012a). Responding to survivors of torture and suffering: Survival skills of Kurdish families. *International Journal of Narrative Therapy and Community Work, 3,* 18–49.

Denborough, D. (2012b). The Team of Life with young men from refugee backgrounds. *International Journal of Narrative Therapy and Community Work, 2,* 44–53.

Denborough, D., Freedman, J., & White, C. (2008). *Strengthening resistance: The use of narrative practices in working with genocide survivors*. Adelaide, Australia: Dulwich Centre Foundation.

Denborough, D., & Preventing Prisoner Rape Project. (2005). Prisoner rape support package. *International Journal of Narrative Therapy and Community Work, 2,* 29–37.

Dulwich Centre. (2000). Living positive lives: A gathering for people living with HIV and workers in the HIV sector, *Dulwich Centre Journal,* 4.

Dulwich Centre. (2008a). Children, parents, and mental health. *International Journal of Narrative Therapy and Community Work, 4,* 3–14.

Dulwich Centre. (2008b). Remembrance: Women and Grief Project. *International Journal of Narrative Therapy and Community Work, 4,* 60–71.

Hedtke, L., & Winslade, J. (2004). *Re-membering lives: Conversations with the dying and the bereaved.* Amityville, NY: Baywood Publishing.

Madigan, S. (2011). *Narrative therapy.* Washington, DC: American Psychological Association.

Mann, S. (2000). Collaborative representation: Narrative ideas in practice. *Gecko: A Journal of Deconstruction and Narrative Ideas in Therapeutic Practice, 2,* 39–49.

Mitchell, S. (2005). Debriefing after traumatic situations: Using narrative ideas in the Gaza Strip. *International Journal of Narrative Therapy and Community Work, 2,* 23–28. Republished in Denborough, D. (Ed.), *Trauma: Narrative responses to traumatic experience.* Adelaide, Australia: Dulwich Centre Publications.

Myerhoff, B. (1982). Life history among the elderly: Performance, visibility, and remembering. In J. Ruby (Ed.), *A crack in the mirror: Reflective perspectives in anthropology* (pp. 99–117). Philadelphia, PA: University of Pennsylvania Press.

O'Leary, P. (1998). Liberation from self-blame: Working with men who have experienced childhood sexual abuse. *Dulwich Centre Journal, 4,* 24–40. Republished 1999 in Dulwich Centre Publications (Eds.), *Extending Narrative Therapy: A collection of practice-based papers* (pp.159–187). Adelaide, Australia: Dulwich Centre Publications.

Rieniets, A. (1995). Souvenir. On *Fluently Helvetica* [CD]. Adelaide, Australia: Independent Production.

Selwyn College, Lewis, D., & Cheshire, A. (1998). Taking the hassle out of school: The work of the Anti-Harassment Team of Selwyn College, Dorothea Lewis & Aileen Cheshire. *Dulwich Centre Journal, 2&3,* 2–31.

Silent Too Long. (2000). Embracing the old, nurturing the new. *Dulwich Centre Journal, 1&2,* 62–71.

Simmons, L. (2007). Stories about home. *International Journal of Narrative Therapy and Community Work, 2,* 26–40.

Sliep, Y., & CARE Counsellors. (1996). Conversations with AIDS and CARE. *Dulwich Centre Newsletter, 3,* 5–11.

Verco, J. (2002). Women's outrage and the pressure to forgive. *International Journal of Narrative Therapy and Community Work, 1,* 23–27. Republished 2003 in Dulwich Centre Publications (Ed.), *Responding to violence: A collection of papers relating to child sexual abuse and violence in intimate relationships* (pp. 119–128). Adelaide, Australia: Dulwich Centre Publications.

Wade, A. (1997). Small acts of living: Everyday resistance to violence and other forms of oppression. *Contemporary Family Therapy, 19*(1), 23–39. Human Sciences Press, Inc.

White, M. (1984). Pseudo-encopresis: From avalanche to victory, from vicious to virtuous cycles. *Family Systems Medicine, 2*(2), 150–160. doi:10.1037/h0091651

White, M. (1988, Spring). Saying hullo again: The incorporation of the lost relationship in the resolution of grief. *Dulwich Centre Newsletter,* 7–11.

White, M. (1994). The narrative perspective in therapy (D. L. Bubenzer, J. D. West, & S. R. Boughner, Interviewers). *Family Journal: Counseling and Therapy for Couples and Families, 2*(1), 71–83. Republished 1995 in M. White, *Re-authoring lives: Interviews and essays* (pp. 11–40). Adelaide, Australia: Dulwich Centre Publications.

White, M. (1995a). Naming abuse and breaking from its effects (C. McLean, Interviewer). In M. White, *Re-authoring lives: Interviews and essays* (pp. 82–111). Adelaide, Australia: Dulwich Centre Publications.

White, M. (1995b). Psychotic experience and discourse (K. Stewart, Interviewer). In M. White, *Re-authoring lives: Interviews and essays* (pp. 112–154). Adelaide, Australia: Dulwich Centre Publications.

White, M. (1997). *Narratives of therapists' lives.* Adelaide, Australia: Dulwich Centre Publications.

White, M. (2002a). Journey metaphors. *International Journal of Narrative Therapy and Community Work, 4,* 12–18. Republished 2004 in,M. White, *Narrative practice and exotic lives: Resurrecting diversity in everyday life* (pp. 43–57). Adelaide: Dulwich Centre Publications.

White, M. (2002b). Addressing personal failure. *International Journal of Narrative Therapy and Community Work, 3,* 33–76. Republished 2004 in M. White, *Narrative practice and exotic lives: Resurrecting diversity in everyday life* (pp. 149–232). Adelaide, Australia: Dulwich Centre Publications.

White, M. (2004a). Narrative practice and the unpacking of identity conclusions. In *Narrative practice and exotic lives: Resurrecting diversity in everyday life* (pp. 119–147). Adelaide, Australia: Dulwich Centre Publications.

White, M. (2004b). Working with people who are suffering the consequences of multiple trauma: A narrative perspective. *International Journal of Narrative Therapy and Community Work, 1,* 45–76. Republished 2006 in D. Denborough (Ed.), *Trauma: Narrative responses to traumatic experience* (pp. 25–85). Adelaide, Australia: Dulwich Centre Publications.

White, M. (2005). Children, trauma and subordinate storyline development. *International Journal of Narrative Therapy and Community Work, 3&4,* 10–22. Republished 2006 in D. Denborough (Ed.), *Trauma: Narrative responses to traumatic experience* (pp. 143–165). Adelaide, Australia: Dulwich Centre Publications.

White, M. (2007). *Maps of narrative practice.* New York, NY: W. W. Norton.

White, C., & Denborough, D. (2005a). Conceptualising conferences as community events. In C. White & D. Denborough (Eds.), *A community of ideas: Behind the scenes: The work of Dulwich Centre Publications* (pp. 45–77). Adelaide, Australia: Dulwich Centre.

White, C., & Denborough, D. (2005b). Letters to ancestry and letters to link communities. In C. White & D. Denborough (Eds.), *A community of ideas: Behind the scenes. The work of Dulwich Centre Publications* (pp. 79–100). Adelaide, Australia: Dulwich Centre.

White, M., & Epston, D. (1990). *Narrative means to therapeutic ends.* New York, NY: W. W. Norton.

White, M., & Epston, D. (1991). A conversation about AIDS and dying. *Dulwich Centre Newsletter, 2,* 7–16. Republished 1992 as in D. Epston & M. White, *Experience, Contradiction, Narrative & Imagination: Selected papers of David Epston & Michael White, 1989–1991* (chapter 2), pp. 27-36.

Wingard, B., & Lester, J. (2001). *Telling our stories in ways that make us stronger.* Adelaide, Australia: Dulwich Centre Publications.

Yuen, A. (2007). Discovering children's responses to trauma: A response-based narrative practice. *International Journal of Narrative Therapy and Community Work, 4,* 3–18.

Index